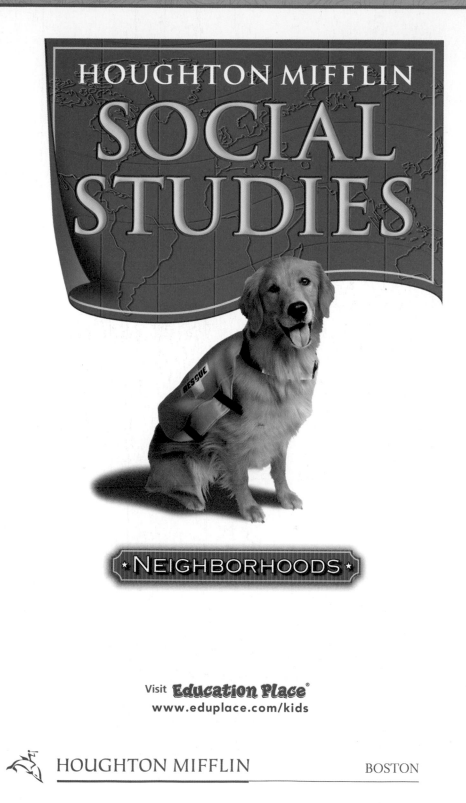

HOUGHTON MIFFLIN
SOCIAL STUDIES

★ NEIGHBORHOODS ★

Visit **Education Place**®
www.eduplace.com/kids

HOUGHTON MIFFLIN   BOSTON

★ AUTHORS ★

Senior Author
Dr. Herman J. Viola
Curator Emeritus
Smithsonian Institution

Dr. Cheryl Jennings
Project Director
Florida Institute of
  Education
University of North
  Florida

Dr. Sarah Witham Bednarz
Associate Professor,
  Geography
Texas A&M University

Dr. Mark C. Schug
Professor and Director
Center for Economic
  Education
University of Wisconsin,
  Milwaukee

Dr. Carlos E. Cortés
Professor Emeritus, History
University of California,
Riverside

Dr. Charles S. White
Associate Professor
School of Education
Boston University

Consulting Authors

Dr. Dolores Beltran
Assistant Professor
Curriculum Instruction
California State University, Los Angeles
(Support for English Language Learners)

Dr. MaryEllen Vogt
Co-Director
California State University Center
for the Advancement of Reading
(Reading in the Content Area)

The United States has honored the Louisiana Purchase and the Lewis and Clark expedition in a new nickel series. The first nickel of the series features a rendition of the Jefferson Peace Medal. Thomas Jefferson commissioned this medal for Lewis and Clark's historic trip, which began in 1804.

HOUGHTON MIFFLIN
SOCIAL STUDIES

★ NEIGHBORHOODS ★

HOUGHTON MIFFLIN   BOSTON

Consultants

Philip J. Deloria
Associate Professor
Department of History
  and Program in
  American Studies
University of Michigan

Lucien Ellington
UC Professor of Education
  and Asia Program
  Co-Director
University of Tennessee,
Chattanooga

Thelma Wills Foote
Associate Professor
University of California,
Irvine

Stephen J. Fugita
Distinguished Professor
Psychology and Ethnic
  Studies
Santa Clara University

Charles C. Haynes
Senior Scholar
First Amendment Center

Ted Hemmingway
Professor of History
The Florida Agricultural &
  Mechanical University

Douglas Monroy
Professor of History
The Colorado College

Lynette K. Oshima
Assistant Professor
Department of Language,
  Literacy and Sociocultural
  Studies and Social Studies
  Program Coordinator
University of New Mexico

Jeffrey Strickland
Assistant Professor, History
University of Texas Pan
  American

Clifford E. Trafzer
Professor of History and
  American Indian Studies
University of California,
Riverside

Teacher Reviewers

Sharon Blount
Meadowbrook
North Kansas City, MO

Jane Cregg
Mendell Elementary
Roxbury, MA

Bonnie Ewing
Ideal Elementary
Countryside, IL

Elizabeth Farrar
Bella Vista School
Bella Vista, CA

Lori Martinez
Woodland Charter
  Elementary
Atlanta, GA

Kathleen Mastaby
Mendell Elementary
Roxbury, MA

Shari Moleterno
Jefferson School
Berwyn, IL

Fred Richardson
West Zephyrhills
  Elementary
Zephyrhills, FL

Phyllis Yamaguchi
Alvarado Elementary
Signal Hill, CA

Donna Zaccaria
William Cramp Elementary
Philadelphia, PA

Printed in the U.S.A.

ISBN: 0-618-42360-5

23456789-VH-13 12 11 10 09 08 07 06 05 04

Contents

Introduction

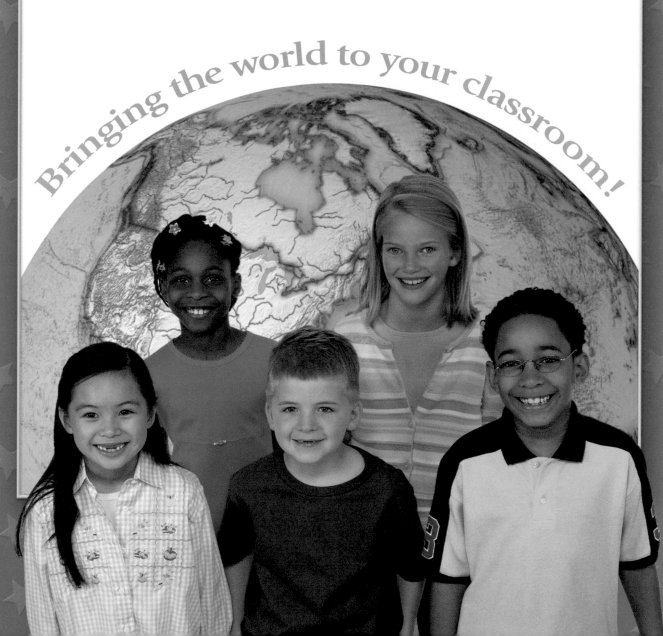

Bringing the world to your classroom!

UNIT 3 Ways of Living 112

6

UNIT 4 | People at Work

Vocabulary Preview
Reading Strategies: Question, Summarize 158

8

UNIT 6 America's Government

278

Vocabulary Preview
Reading Strategies: Summarize, Question

Holidays

9

References

Resources

Extend Lessons

Connect the core lesson to an important concept and dig into it. Extend your social studies knowledge!

Literature

Readers' Theater

Economics

Citizenship

Primary Sources

More primary sources at www.eduplace.com/kids/hmss05/

Geography

Biography

More biographies at www.eduplace.com/kids/hmss05/

History

Skill Lessons

Take a step-by-step approach to learning and practicing key social studies skills.

Map and Globe Skills

Chart and Graph Skills

Study Skills

Citizenship Skills

Reading and Thinking

Reading Skills/Graphic Organizer

N
W E
S

Visual Learning

Maps, graphs, and charts help you learn.

Maps

Charts and Graphs

Diagrams

Timelines

Fine Art

About Your Textbook

① How It's Organized

Units The major sections of your book are units. Each starts with a big idea.

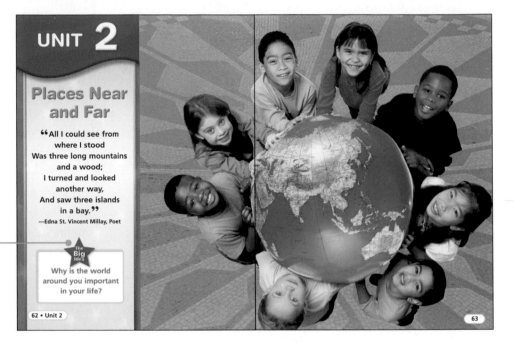

Explore big ideas in geography, history, economics, government, and culture.

Get ready for reading.

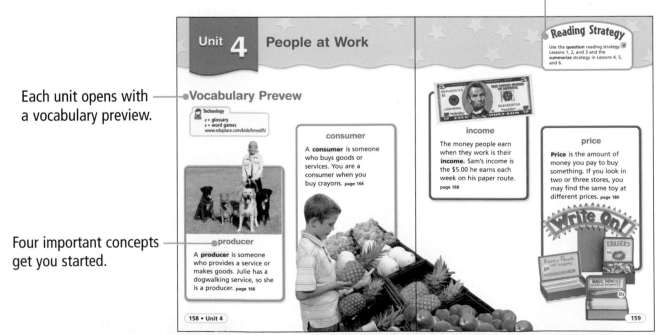

Each unit opens with a vocabulary preview.

Four important concepts get you started.

❷ Core and Extend

Lessons The lessons in your book have two parts: core and extend.

Core Lessons
Lessons bring social studies to life and help you meet your state's standards.

Core Lesson **3**

Extend Lessons
Go deeper into an important topic.

Extend
Primary Sources

Core Lesson

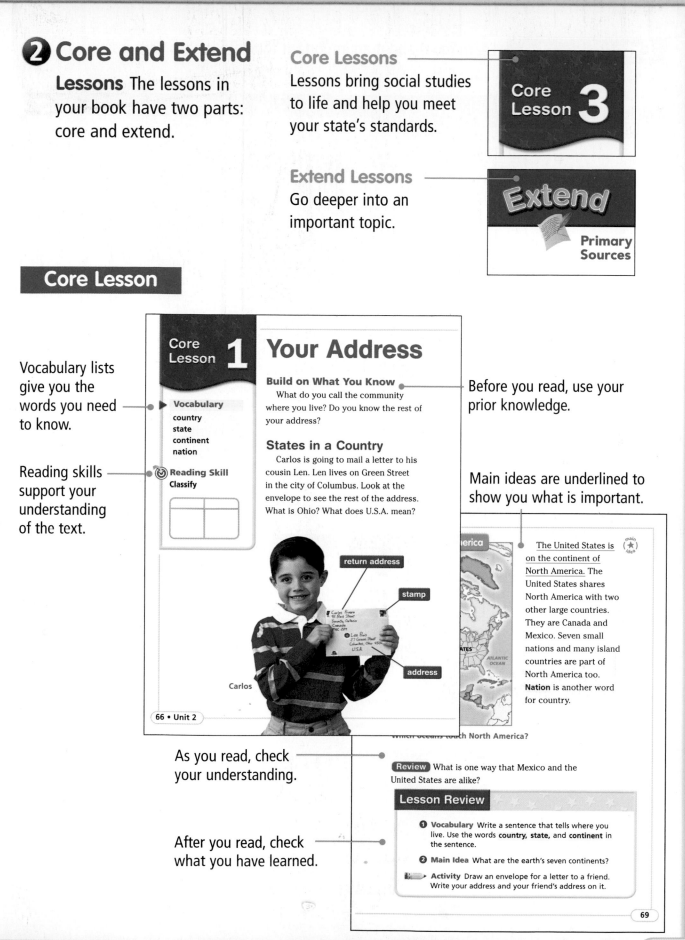

Vocabulary lists give you the words you need to know.

Reading skills support your understanding of the text.

Core Lesson **1** **Your Address**

Build on What You Know
What do you call the community where you live? Do you know the rest of your address?

States in a Country
Carlos is going to mail a letter to his cousin Len. Len lives on Green Street in the city of Columbus. Look at the envelope to see the rest of the address. What is Ohio? What does U.S.A. mean?

▶ **Vocabulary**
country
state
continent
nation

Reading Skill
Classify

return address

stamp

address

Carlos

66 • Unit 2

Before you read, use your prior knowledge.

Main ideas are underlined to show you what is important.

...erica

The United States is on the continent of North America. The United States shares North America with two other large countries. They are Canada and Mexico. Seven small nations and many island countries are part of North America too. **Nation** is another word for country.

ATLANTIC OCEAN

...TES

Which oceans touch North America?

As you read, check your understanding.

After you read, check what you have learned.

Review What is one way that Mexico and the United States are alike?

Lesson Review

❶ **Vocabulary** Write a sentence that tells where you live. Use the words **country, state,** and **continent** in the sentence.

❷ **Main Idea** What are the earth's seven continents?

▶ **Activity** Draw an envelope for a letter to a friend. Write your address and your friend's address on it.

69

Extend Lesson Learn more about an important topic from each core lesson.

Dig in and extend your knowledge.

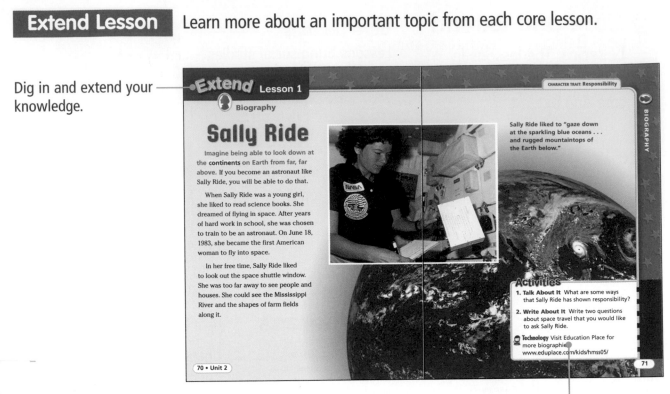

Write, talk, draw, and role-play!

Look for literature, readers' theater, geography, economics—and more.

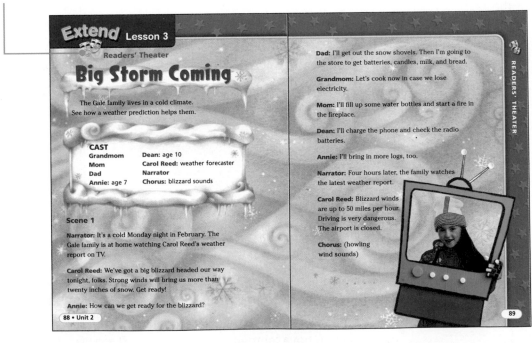

③ Skills

Skill Building
Learn map, graph, and study skills, as well as citizenship skills for life.

Practice and apply each social studies skill.

Skill lessons step it out.

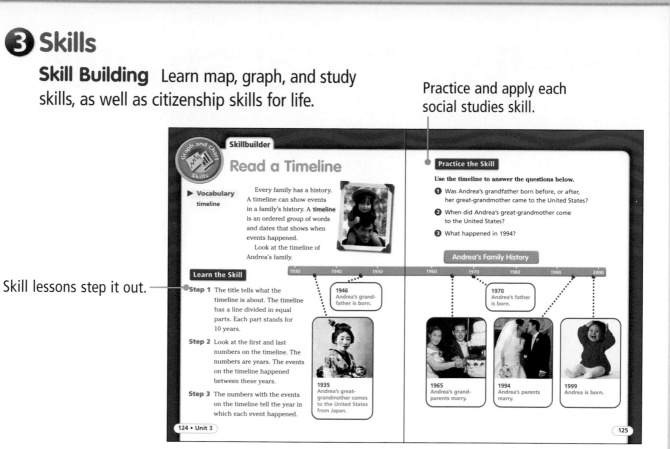

④ References

Citizenship Handbook
The back of your book includes sections you'll refer to again and again.

Resources
Look for atlas maps, a glossary of social studies terms, and an index.

Reading Social Studies

Your book can help you be a successful reader. Here's what you will find:

Preview Learn four important words from the unit.

Lesson Vocabulary Learn the meanings of lesson vocabulary.

Vocabulary Practice Reuse words in the reviews, skills, and extends. Show that you know your vocabulary.

Look through your book and find the reading strategies at the beginning of each unit.

Predict and Infer

Monitor and Clarify

Question

Summarize

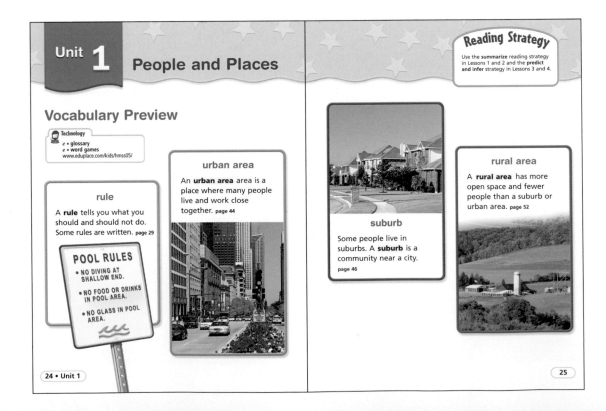

Unit 1 **People and Places**

Reading Strategy

Use the **summarize** reading strategy in Lessons 1 and 2 and the **predict and infer** strategy in Lessons 3 and 4.

Vocabulary Preview

Technology
e • glossary
e • word games
www.eduplace.com/kids/hmss05/

rule

A **rule** tells you what you should and should not do. Some rules are written. page 29

POOL RULES
• NO DIVING AT SHALLOW END.
• NO FOOD OR DRINKS IN POOL AREA.
• NO GLASS IN POOL AREA.

urban area

An **urban area** area is a place where many people live and work close together. page 44

suburb

Some people live in suburbs. A **suburb** is a community near a city. page 46

rural area

A **rural area** has more open space and fewer people than a suburb or urban area. page 52

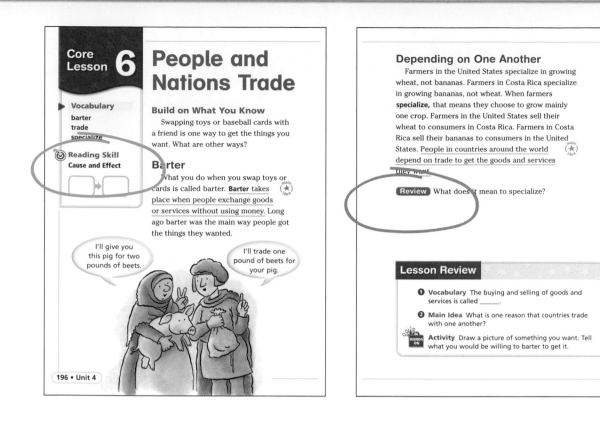

Core Lesson 6

People and Nations Trade

Vocabulary
barter
trade
specialize

Reading Skill
Cause and Effect

Build on What You Know
Swapping toys or baseball cards with a friend is one way to get the things you want. What are other ways?

Barter
What you do when you swap toys or cards is called barter. **Barter** takes place when people exchange goods or services without using money. Long ago barter was the main way people got the things they wanted.

I'll give you this pig for two pounds of beets.

I'll trade one pound of beets for your pig.

196 • Unit 4

Depending on One Another
Farmers in the United States specialize in growing wheat, not bananas. Farmers in Costa Rica specialize in growing bananas, not wheat. When farmers **specialize,** that means they choose to grow mainly one crop. Farmers in the United States sell their wheat to consumers in Costa Rica. Farmers in Costa Rica sell their bananas to consumers in the United States. People in countries around the world depend on trade to get the goods and services they want.

Review What does it mean to specialize?

Lesson Review

❶ **Vocabulary** The buying and selling of goods and services is called _____.

❷ **Main Idea** What is one reason that countries trade with one another?

Activity Draw a picture of something you want. Tell what you would be willing to barter to get it.

199

READING SKILLS

As you read, use the reading skills to organize the information.

Sequence

Cause and Effect

Compare and Contrast

Problem and Solution

Draw Conclusions

Predict Outcomes

Classify

Main Idea and Details

COMPREHENSION SUPPORT

Build on What You Know
Ask yourself what you know about the lesson topic. You may already know a lot!

Review Questions
Answer questions as you read. Did you understand what you read?

Social Studies
Why It Matters

Social Studies is exciting and fun. It is not just a book you read in school. You will use what you learn all your life.

WHEN I
- look around my neighborhood
- or read a map—
  I'll use geography!

WHEN I
- save money or
- decide what to buy—
  I'll use economics!

Town Map

WHEN I
- go to a neighborhood meeting
- or decide who to vote for—
I'll use what I've learned about citizenship!

WHEN I
- hear the story of a person from the past
- read books and visit museums
- look closely at the world around me—
I'll think about history!

UNIT 1

People and Places

"I live in a city, yes I do
I live in a city, yes I do
I live in a city, yes I do
Made by human hands"

—Malvina Reynolds, Poet

The Big Idea

How do land and people make up a community?

Vocabulary Preview

Technology

e • glossary
e • word games
www.eduplace.com/kids/hmss05/

urban area

An **urban area** is a place where many people live and work close together. **page 44**

rule

A **rule** tells you what you should and should not do. Some rules are written. **page 29**

POOL RULES

• NO DIVING AT SHALLOW END.

• NO FOOD OR DRINKS IN POOL AREA.

• NO GLASS IN POOL AREA.

Reading Strategy

Use the **summarize** reading strategy in Lessons 1 and 2 and the **predict and infer** strategy in Lessons 3 and 4.

suburb

Some people live in suburbs. A **suburb** is a community near a city.

page 46

rural area

A **rural area** has more open space and fewer people than a suburb or urban area. page 52

► **Vocabulary**

group
leader
rule

◎ **Reading Skill**

**Compare and
Contrast**

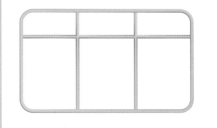

All Kinds of Groups

Build on What You Know

Do you take a class after school? Are you on a team?

Groups

A **group** is a number of people who live together, work together, or spend time together. Your family is a group. Your school class is a group. A church choir is a group too. Families, classes, teams, and choirs are alike because they are groups.

*main
(★)
idea*

Charan belongs to these three groups. What other group or groups do you think he might be in?

Review What groups do you belong to?

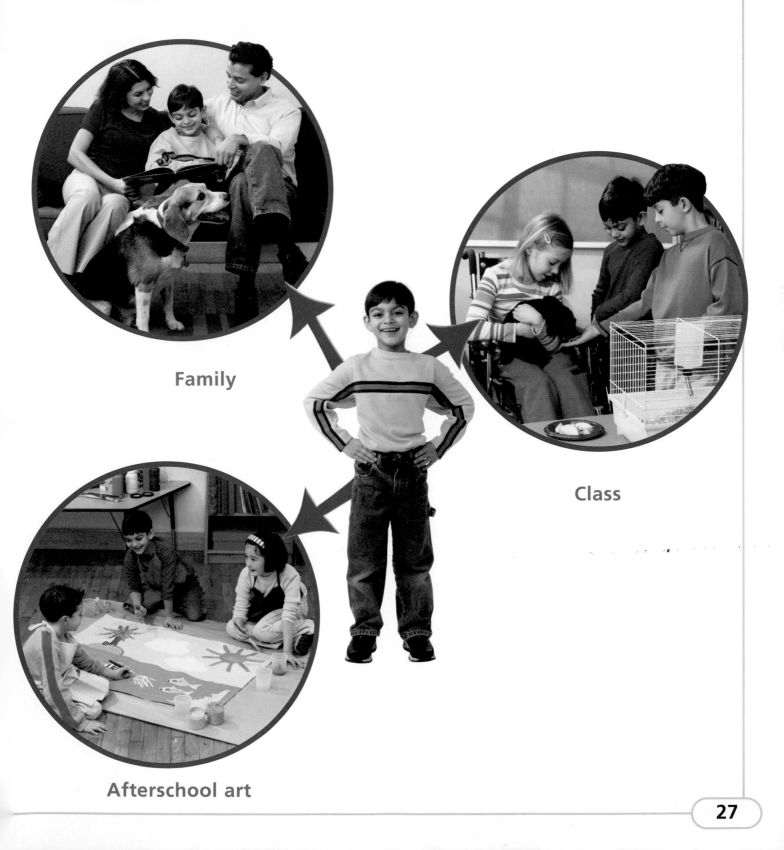

Family

Class

Afterschool art

Leaders

A **leader** is someone who leads others. The leader of a band helps everyone in the band play music together. Teachers are leaders of their classes. In some classrooms, children take turns being leaders of activities or games. Most groups have leaders.

main idea ⭐

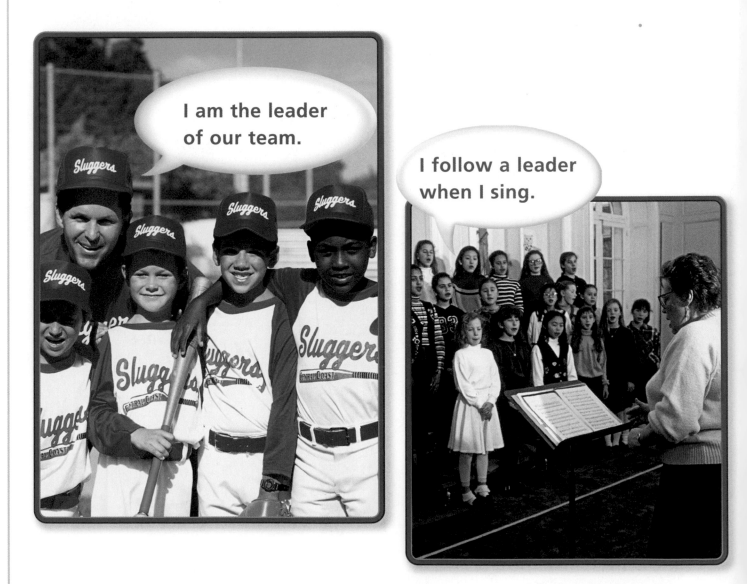

I am the leader of our team.

I follow a leader when I sing.

Rules

A **rule** helps people know what they should and should not do. Most groups have rules. Rules are meant to help people get along. They help people work or play together in the group. Following rules can help the people in a group be safe. In some groups, people talk about their rules. They may make or change their rules together.

Review Why are rules important in a group?

Some groups have a list of printed rules.

Lesson Review

❶ **Vocabulary** Give an example of a **rule** for a **group**.

❷ **Main Idea** Give an example of a group that has a leader. Tell what the leader does.

Activity Think about a group leader that you know. Write or tell what the leader does for the group.

Rules

From the book **Lunch Money and Other Poems About School** by Carol Diggory Shields

Recess Rules

No sliding down the handrails.
No climbing up the slide.
No bouncing on the seesaw.
No throwing sand outside.
No twisting on the swings.
No climbing up the trees.
No jumping from the fences.
No hanging by your knees.

Max slides down the handrails.
He climbs right up the slide.
Max bounces on the seesaw.
He throws the sand outside.
Max twirls the swings up double.
He calls me from a tree.
I climb up. Who gets in trouble?
Max sure doesn't.
Only me.

Activities

1. **Talk About It** Does your school have any recess rules that are not in the poem?

2. **Write About It** Look at the drawing on this page. Write or tell why you think Max does not get in trouble.

Review: Maps and Globes

▶ **Vocabulary**

globe
world map

A **globe** is a model of the earth. It shows that the earth is round like a ball. Maps are drawings of places as seen from above. A **world map** is a flat picture of the earth. You can use a globe and a world map to find continents, oceans, and other places.

Learn the Skill

Step 1 Look at the globe. Oceans are usually colored blue on globes and maps.

Step 2 Find the Atlantic Ocean on the globe and on the world map. In what way is the ocean the same on the map and the globe?

Step 3 Continents are the big bodies of land you see on a globe and a world map. Find North America on the globe and the world map. Globes and maps show countries too. Find Canada on the globe and map.

North Pole

South Pole

Practice the Skill

Look at the globe and the map. Then follow the directions.

 1 Compare the globe and the world map. Tell how they are alike and different.

 2 Look at the globe and find the continent and country where you live. Then find them on the map. Write their names on a sheet of paper.

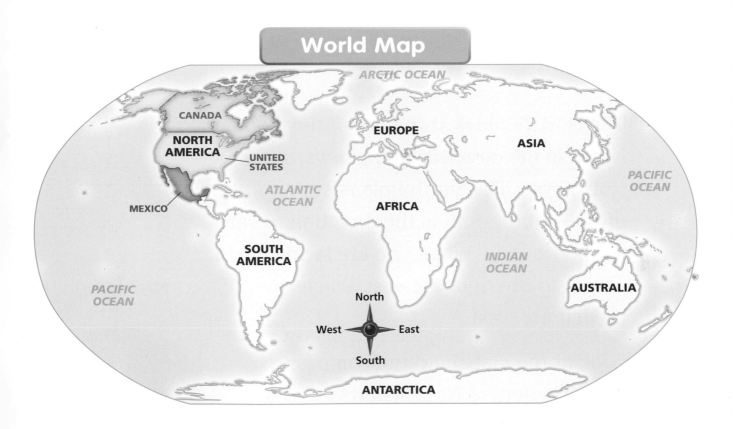

World Map

ARCTIC OCEAN

CANADA

NORTH AMERICA

UNITED STATES

MEXICO

ATLANTIC OCEAN

EUROPE

ASIA

PACIFIC OCEAN

AFRICA

SOUTH AMERICA

INDIAN OCEAN

PACIFIC OCEAN

AUSTRALIA

North

West — East

South

ANTARCTICA

Review: Symbols and Directions

▶ **Vocabulary**

compass rose
symbol

Directions help people find places on globes and maps. A **compass rose** shows directions.

Symbols are pictures that stand for real things. Most maps use symbols. A map key explains what the symbols stand for.

Learn the Skill

N
W —————— E
S

Step 1 The North Pole is at the top of the globe. North is the direction going toward the North Pole. The South Pole is at the bottom of the globe. South is the direction toward the South Pole. When you are facing north, places to the right are east. Places to the left are west.

North Pole

Step 2 Look at the map. Find the compass rose. The letters N, E, S, and W stand for the direction words north, east, south, and west.

Step 3 Look at the map key. The symbol for forest is a tree. Find the symbol for forest on the map.

South Pole

Smithfield

North Road

Smith Road

River Road

Brown Road

Green Road

Forest Road

Map Key

———— Road

🌲🌲 Forest

River

🏠 Farm

Bridge

✈ Airport

North
West — East
South

Practice the Skill

Look at the map. Then follow the directions.

1 Look at the map key. Describe the symbol for road.

2 Find the roads on the map.

3 Look at the river symbol on the map key. Find the river on the map. What is a symbol that touches the river?

4 Use the compass rose and map key to answer the question: What is west of the farm?

Living Together

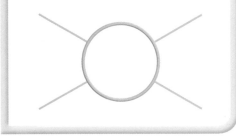
Build on What You Know

Who are some people who live near you? They are your neighbors.

Neighborhoods

You and your neighbors live in a neighborhood. A **neighborhood** is a part of a city or town. Most neighborhoods have homes. Many neighborhoods also have stores, parks, and schools.

main idea

Neighborhood Activities

People in a neighborhood do many things together. Children in a neighborhood may play together. They may go to the same school. The grownups may work together to make their neighborhood look better. People may also work together to make their neighborhood safer.

Review What activities take place in your neighborhood?

What are some places on this map that are in your neighborhood?

Communities

A community is a place where groups of people live. Cities and towns are communities. A community may have a few or many different neighborhoods.

Three Tampa Neighborhoods

Tampa

Northeast Macfarlane

Macfarlane Park

Oakford Park

Hillsborough River

North

West   East

South

Map Key

Northeast Macfarlane

Macfarlane Park

Oakford Park

Park

School

Library

Boys and Girls Club

Skill **Reading Maps** Name the neighborhoods on this map.

People in a Community

People in a community get together for many reasons. Perhaps the community has a fair every year. Often people from different neighborhoods work together to get ready for the event. Others help out on the special day. On Paint Day in Tampa, people work together to help others paint their homes.

Review What are some reasons people get together in communities?

Paint Your Heart Out TAMPA

Lesson Review

❶ **Vocabulary** Explain what a community is.

❷ **Main Idea** What are some ways people work together in neighborhoods and communities?

HANDS ON **Activity** Think about the places you go in your neighborhood. Then draw a picture map that shows those places.

Biography

Maggie Cervantes

Maggie Cervantes (suhr VAHN tays) is a **community** leader in the city of Los Angeles, California. She makes sure that neighbors of all ages meet and help each other. As a child, Cervantes saw that many of her neighbors needed jobs. Some needed better places to live. Cervantes promised herself that some day she would help her community.

Maggie Cervantes as a baby

Maggie Cervantes kept her promise. Today she leads a group that helps people in Los Angeles. Her group helped build safe housing for women and their children. In the buildings are child care centers and places where women learn job skills.

Cervantes says that most of all she loves "bringing people together to get a project done."

Activities

1. **Talk About It** Why did Maggie Cervantes want to help the people in her community?

2. **Write About It** Write or tell two questions you would ask Maggie Cervantes if she visited your class.

Technology Visit Education Place for more biographies. www.eduplace.com/kids/hmss05/

Use a Grid

Grids can help you find places and things on many kinds of maps. A **grid** is a pattern of lines. The lines make columns and rows. Each column has a letter, and each row has a number. The letters and the numbers name each square.

▶ **Vocabulary**

grid

location

Learn the Skill

Step 1 Look at this grid. Put your finger on the star. Move it straight up to the top of the column. What is the letter?

Step 2 Put your finger on the star again. Move it sideways to the beginning of the row. What is the number?

Step 3 Together, the letter and number name the square. The name of the square with the star is B3. That is the place, or **location,** where the star can be found.

Practice the Skill

Look at the map. Then answer the questions.

1 Where is the library located? Name the square.

2 Where is the post office located? Name the square.

3 What is located in square D4?

Cities and Suburbs

Build on What You Know

Maybe you live in a community that has houses with big yards. Or do you live where buildings are close together?

Cities

A city is a place where many people live and work. Cars, trucks, and buses fill the streets. In some urban areas, tall buildings rise into the sky. **Urban area** is another name for city. Buildings are close together in cities. There may be little space for grassy yards. Children play in city parks.

main idea

Skill **Reading Visuals** Compare business centers in two urban areas.

Cities Are Different

main idea

Not all cities are alike. Not even all parts of one city are alike. Often one part of a city has many office buildings close together. Another part of the city may have a zoo, a river, a park, or smaller buildings that are farther apart.

Review What things can you see in urban areas?

Suburbs

Some people live in suburbs. A **suburb** is a community near a city. Spring Valley is a suburb of San Diego.

main idea

Spring Valley has many homes like this one.

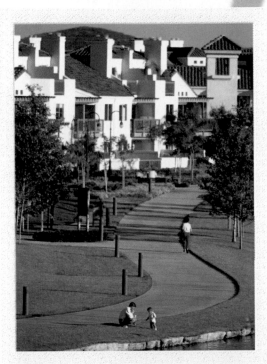

Spring Valley also has apartments and homes like these.

Spring Valley is a big suburb. It has a large amount of land and a large number of people too. In some ways, Spring Valley is like a city. With so many people, Spring Valley needs 18 schools. It has many grocery stores, pizza shops, and other businesses.

Suburbs Depend on Cities

Usually a city has more places to work and shop than any of its suburbs has. Many people who live in suburbs depend on the nearby city for jobs. Also, people come to have fun in a city. People from suburbs all around San Diego can visit the famous San Diego Zoo. Visitors also like Old Town. It shows the way San Diego looked long ago.

main (★) idea

Skill **Reading Maps** Find Spring Valley and San Diego. What other suburbs do you see?

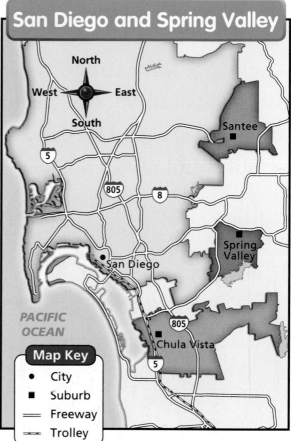

San Diego and Spring Valley

North
West — East
South

Santee

5

805   8

Spring Valley

San Diego

PACIFIC OCEAN

805

Chula Vista

5

Map Key
- • City
- ■ Suburb
- — Freeway
- ⚎ Trolley

Review Compare your community to Spring Valley or San Diego.

Lesson Review

❶ **Vocabulary** Write a sentence that tells two ways that an **urban area** is different from a **suburb.**

❷ **Main Idea** What is one way that a suburb depends on a city?

HANDS ON **Activity** Draw a picture map that shows your community and the nearest city or suburb.

A City Grows Taller

Long ago, New York City was not a city at all. It was a small town. Not far from the center of town, people farmed the land. They grew vegetables and raised animals.

New York once looked like this.

Over the years, more and more people moved to New York. It became a city. In time, the city had a problem. It started to run out of open space.

To solve their problem, New Yorkers began to build skyscrapers. These tall buildings could hold many people and businesses. They used little land space. Today New York City has more than eight million people and many skyscrapers.

Activities

1. **Talk About It** Why did New York City grow taller?

2. **Write About It** Use the words **sky** and **high** to write a poem about a city.

Skillbuilder

Read a Calendar

▶ **Vocabulary**

calendar

Cities and suburbs have community events. A calendar can help citizens keep track of the events. A **calendar** is a way of showing time. A calendar shows months, weeks, and days.

Learn the Skill

Step 1 Name the months of the year in order. Start with January. Then look at the calendar page at right. What month does it show?

Step 2 Each row on the calendar shows one week. Name the seven days of the week. Start with Sunday.

Step 3 Every day of the month has a number, or date. Find the square with the number 6. The date of that day is November 6.

Step 4 Find the community event on the first Saturday of the month. What is it?

Practice the Skill

Look at this community calendar page.
Then answer the questions.

1 What holiday is on November 11?

2 What day of the week is Thanksgiving?

Sunday	Monday	Tuesday	Wednesday	Thursday	Friday	Saturday
			1	2	3	4 Fall Fair
5	6	7 ✓ Election Day	8	9	10	11 Veterans Day
12	13	14	15	16	17	18
19	20	21	22	23 Thanksgiving	24	25
26	27	28	29	30		

NOVEMBER

Rural Communities

Vocabulary

rural area
market

Reading Skill

Compare and
Contrast

Build on What You Know

Do you live on a farm or in a small town? In some ways, your community is different from a city or a suburb.

Small Towns

Outside of cities and suburbs are rural areas. People in rural areas may live in small towns. Small towns have fewer stores, schools, and homes than cities or suburbs have.

main idea

Farms

Rural areas are places with more open space than cities and suburbs. That is why most farms are in rural areas. Farmers need a lot of space to raise animals or crops, such as corn and beans.

The corn that you eat may come from farm fields like this one.

Review Why don't you find farms in cities?

Forests

The wood people use for buildings, chairs, and other things comes from trees. Trees grow in forests. <u>Most forests are found in rural areas</u> because trees need space to grow.

(★) main idea

❶ Lumber companies have workers that cut down trees and saw them into logs.

❷ Logs go to a sawmill to be cut into boards.

❸ Barrels are an example of something that might be made from wood.

Review What are some ways that land is used in rural areas?

Markets

Forest workers and farmers sell their wood and the things they grow. They send those things to markets. A **market** can be anywhere people buy and sell things. People in rural areas may send things they make or grow to markets in cities and suburbs.

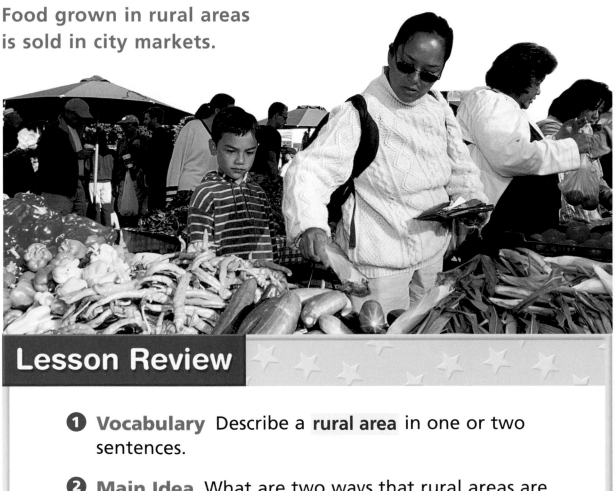

Food grown in rural areas is sold in city markets.

Lesson Review

❶ **Vocabulary** Describe a **rural area** in one or two sentences.

❷ **Main Idea** What are two ways that rural areas are different from urban areas?

Activity Look around your classroom or your home. Make a list of all the things that you see that are made of wood.

Markets

Are you buying? Are you selling? You are in a **market.** In smaller markets, people buy the things they want for their own use. In large markets, businesses buy materials they need to make things. For example, you might have a business that makes chairs. You would go to a big market where many kinds of wood are sold.

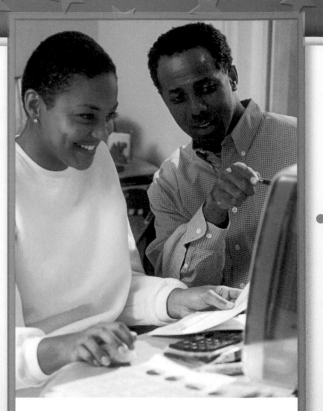

People can buy many different things on an Internet marketplace.

This man sells spices in an open market in Marrakesh, Morocco.

Market

Fishers send their catch to markets like this one in Japan. Here business owners buy large amounts of fish.

A supermarket is filled with many kinds of foods and other things.

Activities

1. **Make It** Make a poster showing the names and prices of some things you would find in a market.

2. **Write About It** Write or tell the kinds of things you would sell if you owned a market.

Big Ideas

Where People Live

Rural Area Suburb Urban Area

Choose the missing words that help describe the chart.

An **1.** _____ has the most buildings and people.

A **2.** _____ is close to a city. A **3.** _____ has the

fewest buildings and people.

Facts and Main Ideas

4. What can leaders do to help a group? (page 28)

5. Why are rules important to a group? (page 29)

6. Why are markets important to people in rural and urban areas? (page 55)

7. What is one way that people can help a community? (pages 37, 39)

Choose the letter of the correct word.

8. A person who leads others

9. Anywhere people buy and sell things

10. Something that tells what people should or should not do

11. A number of people who work, live, or spend time together

12. A place where a group of people live, work, and follow the same rules and laws

> A. **market** (page 55)
>
> B. **rule** (page 29)
>
> C. **community** (page 38)
>
> D. **group** (page 26)
>
> E. **leader** (page 28)

✔ Test Practice

13. What does the word **neighborhood** mean?

    A. a person who leads others

    B. a part of city or town

    C. anywhere that people buy and sell things

    D. something that tells people what to do

Critical Thinking

Compare and Contrast

14. What are some ways that a suburb is the same as a rural area?

Review and Test Prep

Skillbuilders   Use a Grid

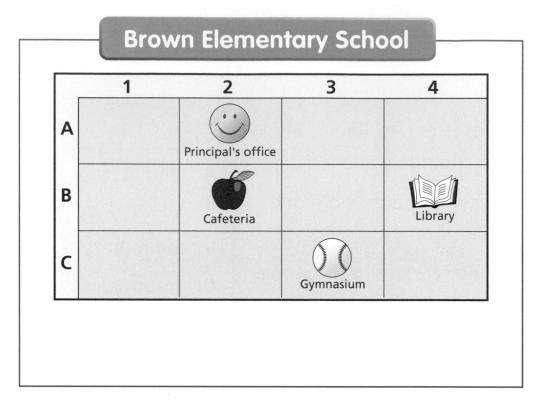

Brown Elementary School

	1	2	3	4
A		Principal's office		
B		Cafeteria		Library
C			Gymnasium	

15. Where is the cafeteria? Use the grid to name the square.

16. What is in square 4B?

Read a Calendar

17. Which holiday is on October 23?

18. What is the date of Columbus Day?

Unit Activity

The Big Idea

Give a Short Report

Choose one of the lessons you have read. Get ready to give a short report about it. Make note cards to help you tell about the lesson.

1 On one card, write something you learned in the lesson.

2 On another card, write or draw something you liked about the lesson.

Our Town is a suburb of San Diego.

Current Events Project

Make a **Leaders in the News** chart. Use information from the Weekly Reader at the Social Studies Website.

LEADER'S NAME	JOB	PLACE

Technology

Current Events Project
For current events information, go to
www.eduplace.com/kids/hmss05/

In Your Classroom

Look for these Social Studies Independent Books in your classroom.

When I Visit My Cousin
by Maggie Cassidy
illustrated by Kathryn Mitter

Jaime Escalante
a Great Teacher
by Carol Peske

Cherry Blossoms Everywhere

At the Library

You may find these books at your school or public library.

On the Town: A Community Adventure
by Judith Caseley

School Rules
by Larry Dane Brimmer

Places Near and Far

"All I could see from where I stood
Was three long mountains and a wood;
I turned and looked another way,
And saw three islands in a bay."

—Edna St. Vincent Millay, Poet

The Big Idea

Why is the world around you important in your life?

Unit 2

Places Near and Far

Vocabulary Preview

Technology

e • **glossary**
e • **word games**
www.eduplace.com/kids/hmss05/

landform

A **landform** is one of the shapes of land found on the earth. One kind of landform is a plain. **page 74**

continent

The United States is on the continent of North America. A **continent** is a large body of land. **page 68**

Reading Strategy

Use the **question** reading strategy in Lessons 1, 2, and 3 and the **monitor and clarify** strategy in Lessons 4 and 5.

climate

Climate is the usual weather of a place over a long time. People in a cold climate need warm homes to live in. page 85

natural resource

Water is an important natural resource. A **natural resource** is something in nature that people use. page 100

Your Address

Build on What You Know

What do you call the community where you live? Do you know the rest of your address?

States in a Country

Carlos is going to mail a letter to his cousin Len. Len lives on Green Street in the city of Columbus. Look at the envelope to see the rest of the address. What is Ohio? What does U.S.A. mean?

▶ **Vocabulary**

country
state
continent
nation

◎ **Reading Skill**

Classify

return address

stamp

Carlos Rivera
95 Rock Street
Toronto, Ontario
Canada
M6C 2J9

Len Ruis
27 Green Street
Columbus, Ohio 430
U.S.A.

address

Carlos

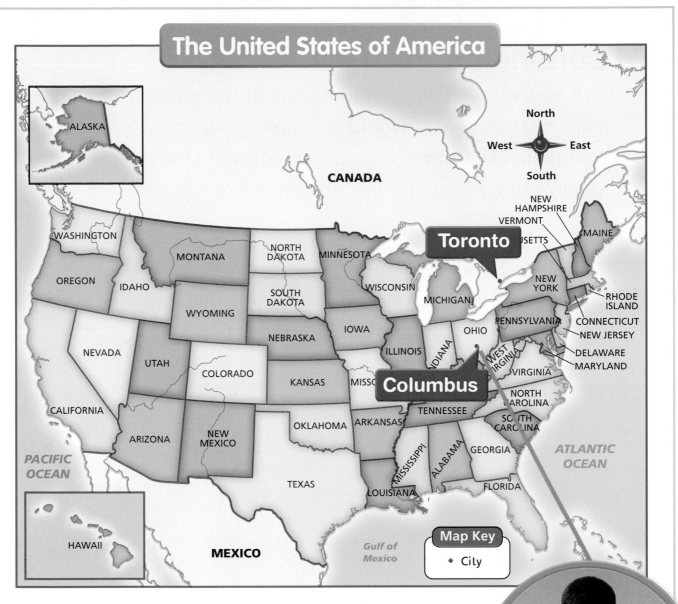

The United States of America

ALASKA

North
West — East
South

CANADA

Toronto

Columbus

NEW HAMPSHIRE
VERMONT
MAINE
USETTS
NEW YORK
RHODE ISLAND
PENNSYLVANIA
CONNECTICUT
NEW JERSEY
DELAWARE
MARYLAND
WEST VIRGINIA
VIRGINIA
NORTH CAROLINA
SOUTH CAROLINA
GEORGIA

WASHINGTON
OREGON
IDAHO
MONTANA
NORTH DAKOTA
MINNESOTA
WISCONSIN
MICHIGAN
SOUTH DAKOTA
WYOMING
NEBRASKA
IOWA
ILLINOIS
INDIANA
OHIO
NEVADA
UTAH
COLORADO
KANSAS
MISSO
TENNESSEE
CALIFORNIA
ARIZONA
NEW MEXICO
OKLAHOMA
ARKANSAS
MISSISSIPPI
ALABAMA
TEXAS
LOUISIANA
FLORIDA

PACIFIC OCEAN

ATLANTIC OCEAN

HAWAII

MEXICO

Gulf of Mexico

Map Key
• City

The city of Columbus is in the state of Ohio.

The letters U.S.A. on the envelope stand for the country called the United States of America. A **country** is a land where people have the same laws and leaders. Ohio is a state in the United States. A **state** is a part of a country. The United States is a country made up of 50 states.

Len

main
(★)
idea

Review Which state do you live in?

Continents

If you were an astronaut looking at the earth from a space station, you would see mostly oceans. You would also see some very large bodies of land. Most of those large bodies of land are **continents.**

main idea (★)

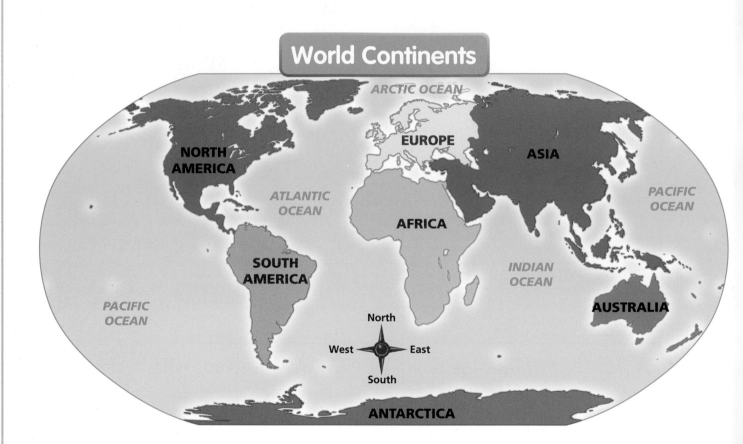

World Continents

ARCTIC OCEAN

EUROPE

ASIA

NORTH AMERICA

ATLANTIC OCEAN

PACIFIC OCEAN

AFRICA

SOUTH AMERICA

INDIAN OCEAN

PACIFIC OCEAN

North

West — East

South

AUSTRALIA

ANTARCTICA

Skill **Reading Maps** Find and name the seven continents on the map. Find and name the four oceans.

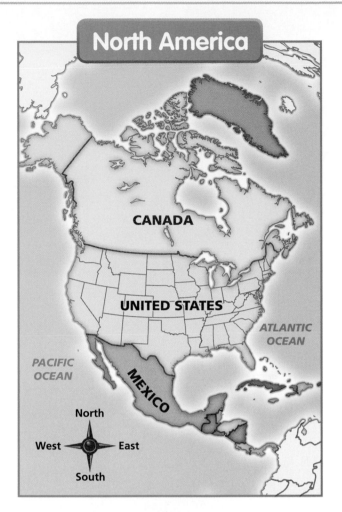

North America

The United States is *main idea* ⭐

on the continent of

North America. The United States shares North America with two other large countries. They are Canada and Mexico. Seven small nations and many island countries are part of North America too. **Nation** is another word for country.

Which oceans touch North America?

Review What is one way that Mexico and the United States are alike?

Lesson Review

❶ **Vocabulary** Write a sentence that tells where you live. Use the words **country**, **state**, and **continent** in the sentence.

❷ **Main Idea** What are the earth's seven continents?

✏️ **Activity** Draw an envelope for a letter to a friend. Write your address and your friend's address on it.

Sally Ride

Imagine being able to look down at the continents on Earth from far, far above. If you become an astronaut like Sally Ride, you will be able to do that.

When Sally Ride was a young girl, she liked to read science books. She dreamed of flying in space. After years of hard work in school, she was chosen to train to be an astronaut. On June 18, 1983, she became the first American woman to fly into space.

In her free time, Sally Ride liked to look out the space shuttle window. She was too far away to see people and houses. She could see the Mississippi River and the shapes of farm fields along it.

Sally Ride liked to "gaze down at the sparkling blue oceans . . . and rugged mountaintops of the Earth below."

Activities

1. **Talk About It** What are some ways that Sally Ride has shown responsibility?

2. **Write About It** Write two questions about space travel that you would like to ask Sally Ride.

Technology Visit Education Place for more biographies. www.eduplace.com/kids/hmss05/

Map and Globe Skills

Parts of a Globe

To show locations on a globe, we use the **poles,** the **equator,** and **hemispheres.**

▶ **Vocabulary**

pole
equator
hemisphere

Learn the Skill

The North and South poles are imaginary. You cannot see them on the earth, only on a globe.

North Pole

South Pole

Step 1 The equator is an imaginary line around the middle of the earth. It is halfway between the North Pole and the South Pole.

Step 2 The equator divides the earth into the Northern Hemisphere and the Southern Hemisphere.

Step 3 The maps on page 72 show that the earth may also be divided into Eastern and Western hemispheres.

Practice the Skill

Look at the maps. Then follow the directions.

1 Find the continent where you live. Tell which hemispheres you live in.

2 Which continent has land in all four hemispheres?

3 Name two continents in the Southern Hemisphere.

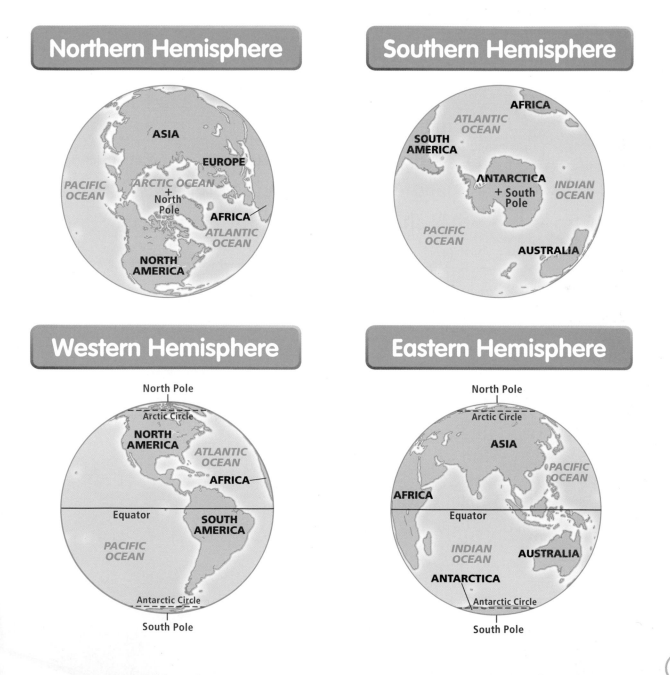

Northern Hemisphere

ASIA
EUROPE
ARCTIC OCEAN
+ North Pole
PACIFIC OCEAN
AFRICA
ATLANTIC OCEAN
NORTH AMERICA

Southern Hemisphere

AFRICA
ATLANTIC OCEAN
SOUTH AMERICA
ANTARCTICA
+ South Pole
INDIAN OCEAN
PACIFIC OCEAN
AUSTRALIA

Western Hemisphere

North Pole
Arctic Circle
NORTH AMERICA
ATLANTIC OCEAN
AFRICA
Equator
SOUTH AMERICA
PACIFIC OCEAN
Antarctic Circle
South Pole

Eastern Hemisphere

North Pole
Arctic Circle
ASIA
PACIFIC OCEAN
AFRICA
Equator
INDIAN OCEAN
AUSTRALIA
ANTARCTICA
Antarctic Circle
South Pole

Land and Water

▶ Vocabulary

landform
valley
island
peninsula
lake

Ⓜ Reading Skill

**Compare and
Contrast**

Build on What You Know

Think about your community. Is it flat? Is it hilly? Is there a body of water nearby?

Landforms

The land on the earth is shaped in many different ways. Each different shape, such as a hill or mountain, is a **landform.** The pictures on pages 74 to 79 show some different landforms.

main idea

Sierra Nevada in California

mountains

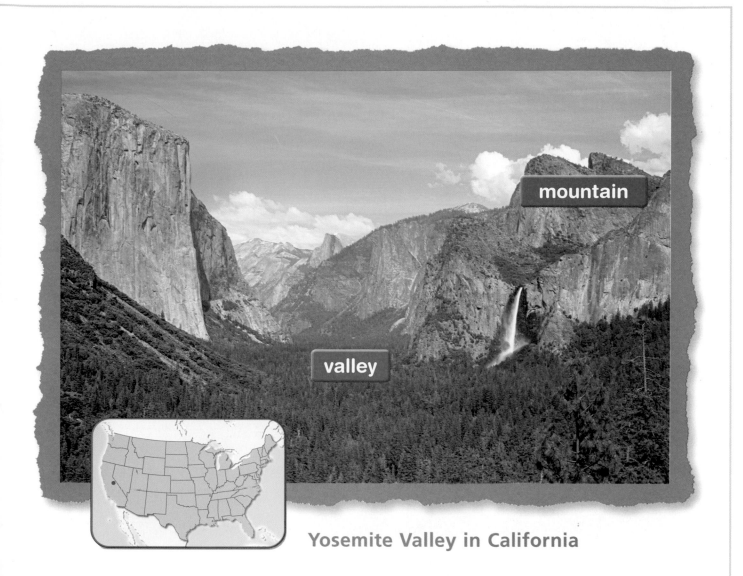

mountain

valley

Yosemite Valley in California

A **valley** is low land between mountains or hills. Often a valley has been carved out by a river running through it. More people choose to farm in valleys than on the steep sides of mountains.

Review Why do you think people are more likely to farm in valleys than in mountains?

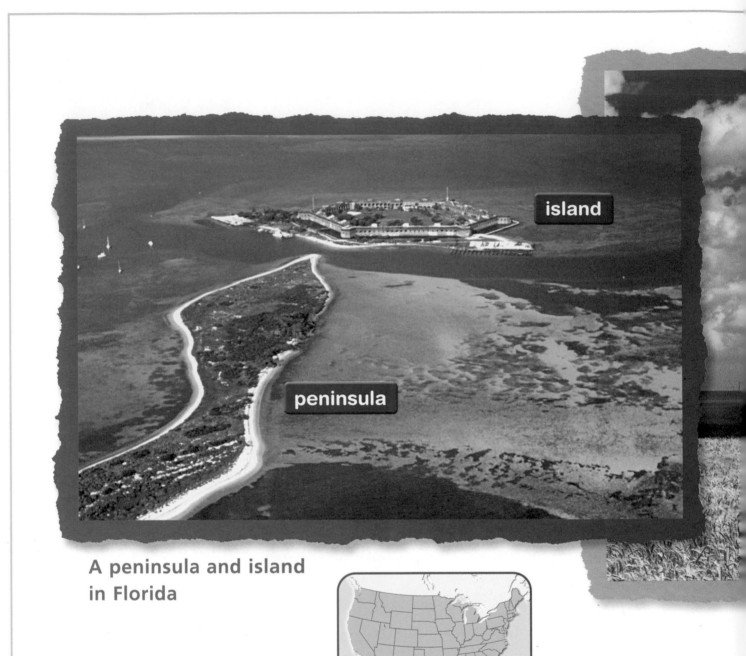

A peninsula and island in Florida

Islands and peninsulas are a little alike. An **island** is land with water all around it. A **peninsula** is land that has water on three sides. Most of the state of Florida is a peninsula. The Delmarva Peninsula has parts of Maryland and Virginia and all of Delaware.

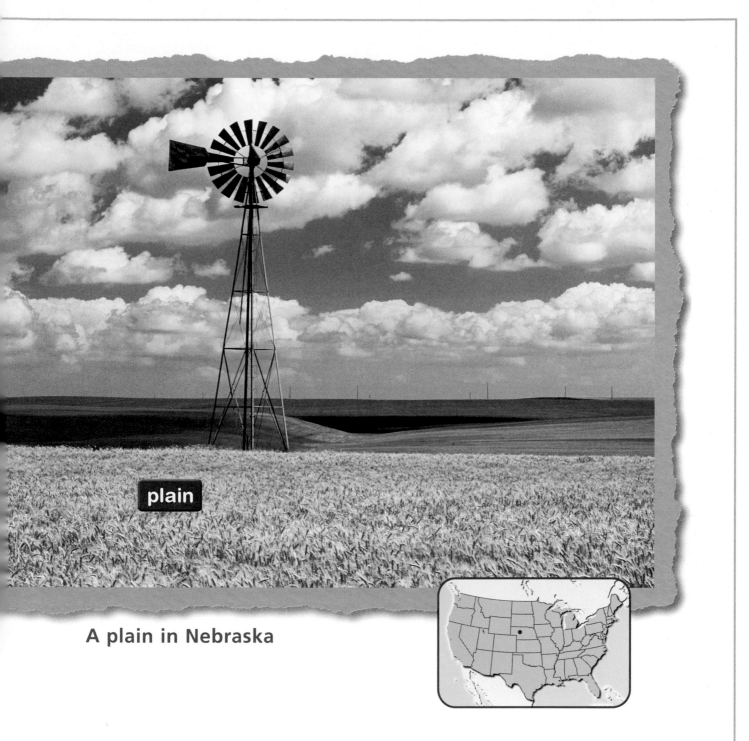

plain

A plain in Nebraska

A plain is mostly flat land. Most of the middle of the United States is covered by plains. Other plains are found on the land along the Atlantic Ocean and the Gulf of Mexico.

Review What is one landform in your state?

Water

Water comes in many shapes and forms too. You have read that most of the earth is covered with ocean water. Ocean water is salty. Most bodies of water found on land have fresh water.

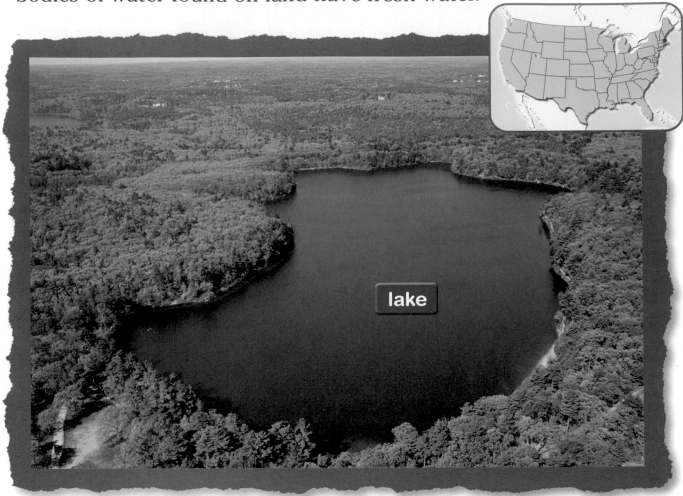

A lake in Massachusetts

A **lake** is a body of water with land all around it. Most lakes have fresh water. Lakes come in many sizes. Some are small mountain lakes. Others, like Lake Superior, are huge. Find Lake Superior and the other four Great Lakes on a map of the United States.

river

The Allegheny and Monongahela rivers meet at Pittsburgh, Pennsylvania.

A river is a long, moving body of fresh water. Rivers flow downhill into oceans, or lakes, or other rivers.

Review What is a difference between an ocean and most lakes?

Lesson Review

❶ **Vocabulary** Write one or two sentences that tell what you know about **landforms.**

❷ **Main Idea** What are some kinds of land and water on the earth?

HANDS ON **Activity** Draw a picture of how people use land and water in your community.

The Great Smokies

A legend is a story that is told and retold over many, many years. Joseph Bruchac retold this Cherokee legend about **landforms.**

If we should travel
far to the South,
there in the land
of mountains and mist,
we might hear the story
of how Earth was first shaped.

Water Beetle came out
to see if it was ready,
but the ground was
still as wet as a swamp,
too soft for anyone to stand.

Great Buzzard said, "I will help dry the land."
He began to fly close above the new Earth.
Where his wings came down,
valleys were formed,
and where his wings lifted,
hills rose up through the mist.

So the many rolling valleys and hills
of that place called the Great Smokies
came into being there.

Activities

1. **Talk About It** How does the Cherokee legend say that valleys were formed?

2. **Write About It** Make up a story about how another landform came to be.

Use Intermediate Directions

▶ **Vocabulary**

northeast
southeast
southwest
northwest

When people travel from one city to another they often use maps to find their way. A compass rose shows them the directions.

Learn the Skill

Look at the compass rose below.

Step 1 Point to the directions north, south, east, and west. The letters N, S, E, and W stand for each direction word.

Step 2 Find the line halfway between north and east. This line points in the direction called **northeast.**

Step 3 Now find the line halfway between south and west. This line points in the direction called **southwest.**

Step 4 Find the letters NE, SE, SW, and NW. These letters stand for the direction words **northeast, southeast, southwest,** and **northwest.**

Look at the map. Then follow the directions.

1 Find Gettysburg, Pennsylvania. In what direction do you go to get to Selma, Alabama?

2 Find Columbus, Ohio. What direction do you go to get to St. Paul, Minnesota?

3 Leave Santa Fe, New Mexico, and travel northeast. Which city on this map do you reach first?

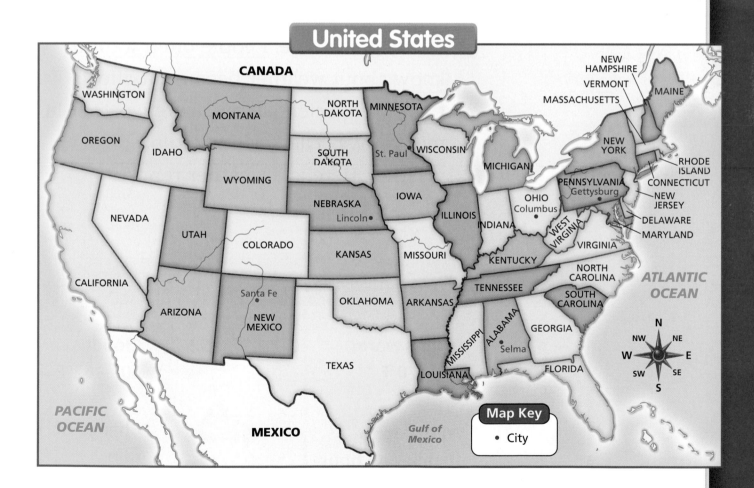

United States

Weather and Climate

Build on What You Know

Is it raining, snowing, or sunny today? What it is like outside makes a difference in the activities you do each day.

Weather

Weather is what the air is like outside at any given time. <u>People often want to know about weather because it affects their lives.</u> Scientists measure weather in many ways. They also try to predict weather. Here is a weather report.

main idea

Today	Tomorrow
Sunny, warm 65° – 70°F	Cloudy 60° – 62°F
Winds up to 10 miles an hour	Chance of rain

Skill **Chart Reading** What do the words, numbers, and pictures tell about weather?

Climate

Climate is the usual weather of a place over a long time. A climate can have different kinds of weather. Jim and Jenna tell about the climate where they live.

July can be very hot in Milwaukee, Wisconsin.
Jim

January can be really cold.
Jim

Mobile, Alabama, has warm weather most of the year.
Jenna

Rain storms are part of our climate too.
Jenna

Review What are two kinds of weather that could be in one climate?

85

Living in Different Climates

Climates make a difference in the way people live. main idea

In what ways are these two climates different?

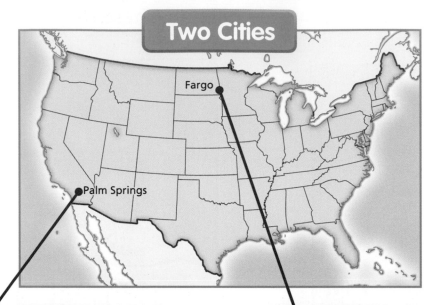

Two Cities

Fargo

Palm Springs

Palm Springs, California
has a climate that is hot and dry in daytime.

People need:
- cool air in buildings and cars year round
- light clothes to wear

Fargo, North Dakota
has a climate that is very cold in winter.

People need:
- warm air in buildings and cars in winter
- clothes to keep out snow and cold

Cold Climate Job
How do you know that this picture was not taken in Palm Springs?

Farmers raise plants and animals that do well in their climate. Builders think of climate when they plan homes and other buildings. Also, some jobs fit one climate and not another. Driving a snowplow is one example. Mostly, though, people have found ways to live in almost all climates.

Review What is one way that climate makes a difference in what people do?

Lesson Review

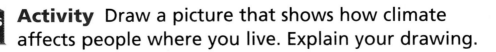

❶ **Vocabulary** Write sentences to explain the difference between **weather** and **climate.**

❷ **Main Idea** Explain how weather and climate are related.

Activity Draw a picture that shows how climate affects people where you live. Explain your drawing.

Big Storm Coming

The Gale family lives in a cold climate.
See how a weather prediction helps them.

CAST

Grandmom	**Dean:** age 10
Mom	**Carol Reed:** weather forecaster
Dad	**Narrator**
Annie: age 7	**Chorus:** blizzard sounds

Scene 1

Narrator: It's a cold Monday night in February. The Gale family is at home watching Carol Reed's weather report on TV.

Carol Reed: We've got a big blizzard headed our way tonight, folks. Strong winds will bring us more than twenty inches of snow. Get ready!

Annie: How can we get ready for the blizzard?

Dad: I'll get out the snow shovels. Then I'm going to the store to get batteries, candles, milk, and bread.

Grandmom: Let's cook now in case we lose electricity.

Mom: I'll fill up some water bottles and start a fire in the fireplace.

Dean: I'll charge the phone and check the radio batteries.

Annie: I'll bring in more logs, too.

Narrator: Four hours later, the family watches the latest weather report.

Carol Reed: Blizzard winds are up to 50 miles per hour. Driving is very dangerous. The airport is closed.

Chorus: (howling wind sounds)

Scene 2

Narrator: The family is watching the weather report on Wednesday afternoon.

Carol Reed: We now have 33 inches of snow. This is the worst blizzard in ten years!

Dad: I'm glad we got our supplies ready.

Grandmom: Yes! The electricity was out for nine hours.

Annie: Toasting marshmallows in the fireplace was fun!

Grandmom: Once when I was a girl, I was stuck at school overnight. A big storm surprised us, and no one could travel. People couldn't predict the weather very well then.

Dad: Predictions are much better today.

Mom: Carol Reed predicted this one right.

Dean: I predict we'll dig lots of snow tomorrow.

Annie: Let's make a whole bunch of snow people, too! I wonder if school's going to be closed again?

Carol Reed: The snow should stop late tonight, but most schools will be closed tomorrow. Check the list on your screen.

Annie: Look! Our school's on the list!

Carol Reed: See you tonight at six!

Chorus: (howling wind sounds)

Activities

1. **Talk About It** Tell ways that weather prediction helps people.

2. **Write About It** Write or tell about a storm that you know about. Tell what people did to stay safe.

Regions

Build on What You Know

Think about your neighborhood. What makes it different from a nearby neighborhood?

Regions

A **region** is an area that has some (★ main idea). shared natural or human feature. People use regions as a way of describing places. Some regions are natural regions such as climate, landform, or plant regions. Other regions are human regions. They are described by human features. The languages that people speak and the work they do are two human features.

Mountains

Highlands

Landform Regions

Areas with shared landforms are landform regions. The United States has many landform regions. The map shows the main ones.

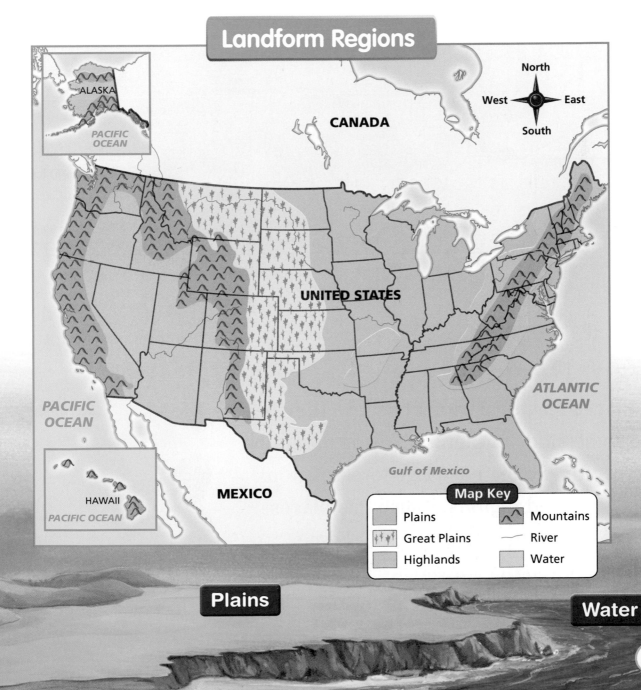

main idea ★

Review What is one landform region that your state has?

Skill **Reading Maps** Which part of the United States has more mountains, eastern or western?

Landform Regions

ALASKA

PACIFIC OCEAN

North
West — East
South

CANADA

UNITED STATES

PACIFIC OCEAN

HAWAII
PACIFIC OCEAN

MEXICO

Gulf of Mexico

ATLANTIC OCEAN

Map Key

Plains

Great Plains

Highlands

Mountains

River

Water

Plains

Water

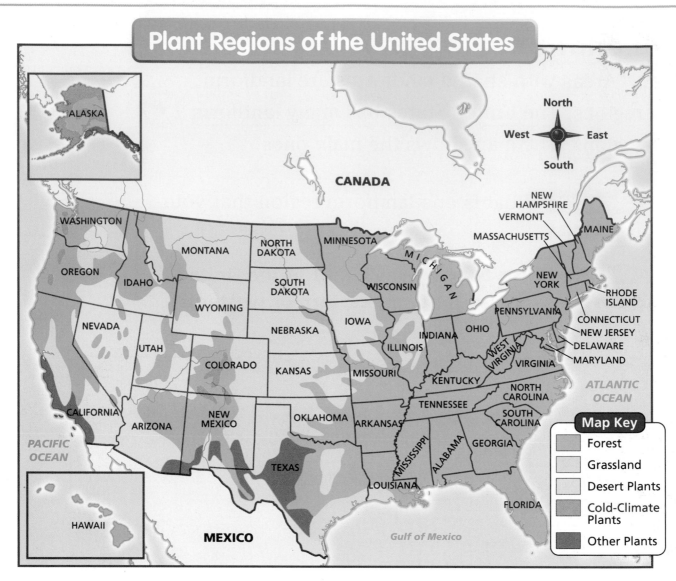

Plant Regions of the United States

ALASKA

North
West — East
South

CANADA

WASHINGTON
MONTANA
NORTH DAKOTA
MINNESOTA
NEW HAMPSHIRE
VERMONT
MAINE
MASSACHUSETTS
OREGON
IDAHO
SOUTH DAKOTA
WISCONSIN
MICHIGAN
NEW YORK
RHODE ISLAND
WYOMING
PENNSYLVANIA
CONNECTICUT
NEVADA
NEBRASKA
IOWA
OHIO
NEW JERSEY
UTAH
ILLINOIS
INDIANA
WEST VIRGINIA
DELAWARE
MARYLAND
COLORADO
KANSAS
MISSOURI
VIRGINIA
CALIFORNIA
KENTUCKY
ATLANTIC OCEAN
NORTH CAROLINA
TENNESSEE
ARIZONA
NEW MEXICO
OKLAHOMA
ARKANSAS
SOUTH CAROLINA
PACIFIC OCEAN
MISSISSIPPI
ALABAMA
GEORGIA
TEXAS
LOUISIANA
FLORIDA
HAWAII
MEXICO
Gulf of Mexico

Map Key
- Forest
- Grassland
- Desert Plants
- Cold-Climate Plants
- Other Plants

Which states have desert plants?

Prickly pear cactus, a desert plant

Plant Regions

Places may be regions because they have main (★) idea the same kinds of plants growing naturally. The United States has large forest regions and grassland regions. It also has places where few kinds of plants grow. Some places are too dry for most plants. Other places are too cold and windy.

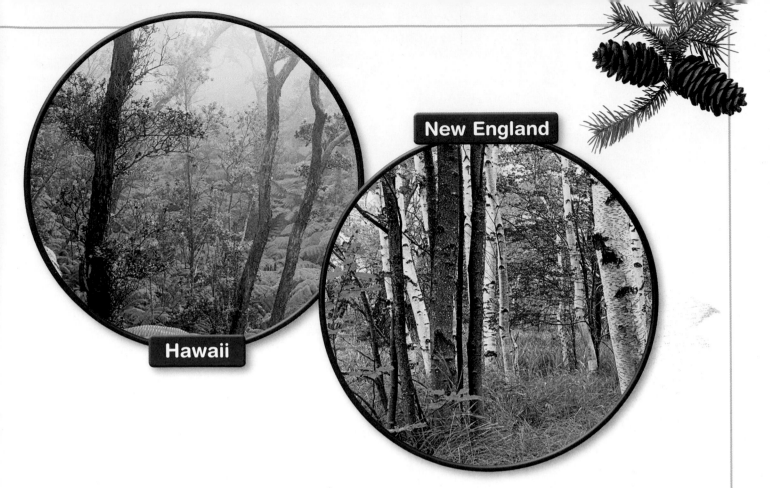

New England

Hawaii

The United States has many kinds of forests. The
forest on the left has the kinds of trees that grow in
the hot climate of Hawaii. The forest on the right
has the kinds of trees that grow in New England's
cool climate.

Review What are two kinds of plant regions?

Lesson Review

❶ **Vocabulary** Describe one kind of landform **region.**

❷ **Main Idea** What region do you live in?

HANDS ON **Activity** Use the map on page 94. Draw a picture of
the kinds of plants that grow naturally in your region.

Languages of Switzerland

One day Marie visited a city in Switzerland called Genf. At the same time, her friend Sam visited Genève, and her friend Kim went to Ginevra. Surprise! They all met in the same city! How can a city have more than one name?

Switzerland is a small country, but it has four national languages. In the past, people in each **region** spoke a different language. Today, the regions are not as clear. Most people in Switzerland speak more than one language. Still, many signs say the same thing in three or four languages.

SWITZERLAND

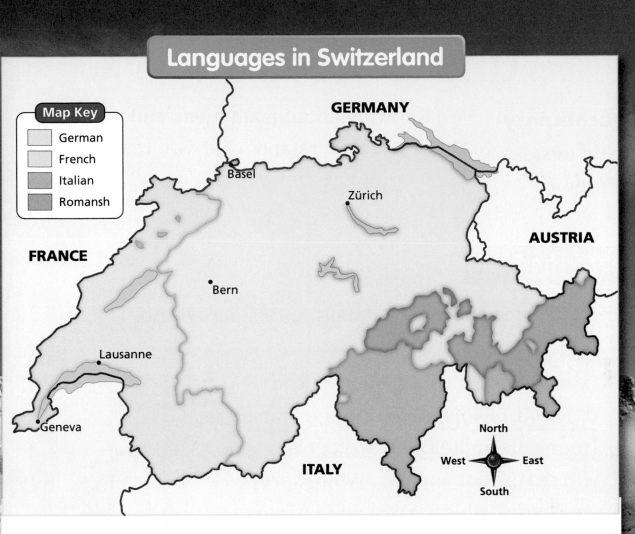

Languages in Switzerland

Map Key
- German
- French
- Italian
- Romansh

GERMANY

FRANCE

AUSTRIA

Basel

Zürich

Bern

Lausanne

Geneva

ITALY

North
West — East
South

Skill **Reading Maps** Which language is spoken in most of Switzerland?

Activities

1. **Read a Map** Which is the second largest language region in Switzerland?

2. **Write About It** Explain how Marie, Sam, and Kim could go to Genf, Genève, and Ginevra and still be in the same city.

Skillbuilder

Identify Main Idea and Details

▶ **Vocabulary**

main idea

detail

Knowing about main ideas and details can help you understand what you read.

Learn the Skill

Look for the **main idea** and **details** in this paragraph.

> Different kinds of trees grow in different regions of the United States. Honey mesquite (meh SKEET) trees grow where it is hot and dry. White spruce trees grow where it is cold in winter. Live oak trees grow in warm, wet regions.

main (★) *idea*

Step 1 The main idea tells what the whole paragraph is about. In this paragraph, the first sentence tells the main idea. But the main idea can be any sentence that tells what the whole paragraph is about.

Step 2 The other sentences in this paragraph give the details. Each detail tells more about the main idea.

Live oak leaves and acorns

Practice the Skill

Read the paragraph below and look at the map.

1 Tell the main idea of this paragraph.

2 Give one detail from the paragraph and one detail from the map that tell more about the main idea.

Some regions of the United States get more rain than others. It rains the most on the northwest coast of the United States. The southeast region gets a lot of rain, too. The region that gets the least rain is the southwest.

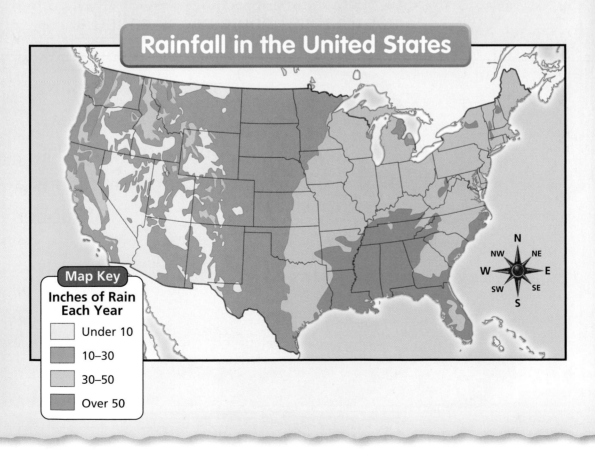

Rainfall in the United States

Map Key

Inches of Rain Each Year

- Under 10
- 10–30
- 30–50
- Over 50

Resources

Vocabulary

natural resource
environment

Reading Skill

Sequence

Build on What You Know

Do you have plants in your classroom? What do plants need to grow? Most plants need air, soil, water, and sunlight. These things are all found in nature. People did not make them.

Different Kinds of Resources

People use different kinds of resources. Like plants, people use things from nature. Something in nature that people use is called a **natural resource.** Air, soil, and water are natural resources. So are trees, rocks, oil, and some kinds of rubber.

main idea

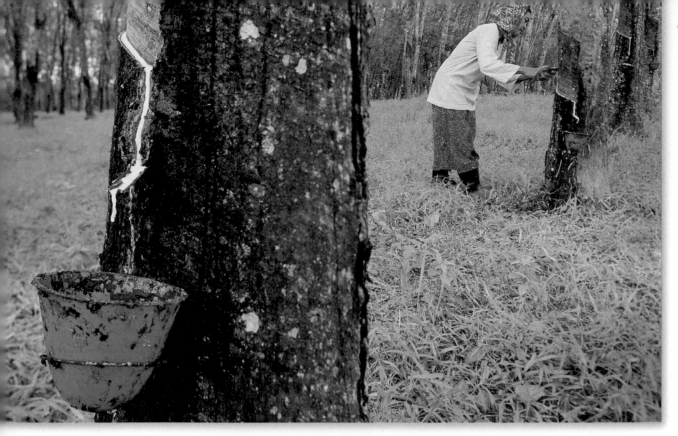

A woman cuts grooves in the bark of rubber trees to get the liquid from which natural rubber is made.

Two Kinds of Rubber

At one time, people had only natural rubber. They made it from a liquid found in some trees. Then scientists found a way to make rubber in their labs. This kind of rubber is called synthetic (sihn THET ihk) rubber. It is an example of another kind of resource. It is a synthetic resource. A synthetic resource is made from materials that people make, not from natural materials.

main idea ★

Review Resources may be found in nature. What is another way people get resources?

Can People Get More of It?

Some natural resources can be replaced. Others cannot be replaced. If you cut down a tree, you can plant another one. But if you keep pumping oil out of a well, someday it will run dry. You cannot get more oil from the same place. You might look for oil somewhere else.

main ★ idea

Resources that can be replaced

Trees

Resources that cannot be replaced

Oil

Review What is another resource that can be replaced?

Changing the Environment

main (★) idea

The natural world around you is called the environment. Land, water, plants, animals, and people are all part of the environment. People change their environment. To build many homes, roads, and businesses, they cut down trees or smooth away hills. People drill wells for water, build dams across rivers, and drain swamps.

Frame a house.

Cut the trees.

Clear the land.

Consequences

main idea ★

Everything people do to the land and resources has a consequence. For example, one important resource in our environment is plants. The roots of trees and other plants help hold the soil down. If you cut down trees, the soil may blow away in the wind. Rain may wash away soil. Losing soil is a consequence of peoples' actions.

People have planted trees to replace some of the ones they cut down.

People recycle paper, plastic, and metals to save resources.

In the past, people did many things to hurt the environment. Some countries made laws to protect the environment. People had to start to clean up the land and water. They had to find ways to keep the air and water clean. Because of the laws and people's actions, some parts of our environment are cleaner than they used to be.

Lesson Review

1 Vocabulary Write a sentence explaining how you use a **natural resource.**

2 Main Idea How are synthetic and natural resources different?

Activity Write or tell about something that you can do to help take care of the environment.

Maple Talk

Think of ways that trees are natural resources. Read about natural resources in the poem "Maple Talk" from **Poems Have Roots** by Lilian Moore.

Plant us.
Let our roots go
deeply down.
We'll hold the soil
when rain tugs
at the earth.

Plant us.
You will better know
how seasons come
and go.

Watch for
    our leaves unfurling
    in spring green,
    our leafy roofs of summer
    over pools of shade
    our sunset red and gold
    igniting autumn's blaze.

When cold winds
leave us bare
we'll show you treetop nests
where songbirds hid
their young.

And when
in early spring
the sweet sap flows again,
have syrup for your pancakes!

Plant us.

Activities

1. **Talk About It** What are two ways that the maple tree is useful to people?

2. **Make a List** Find as many natural resources in the poem as you can.

Big Ideas

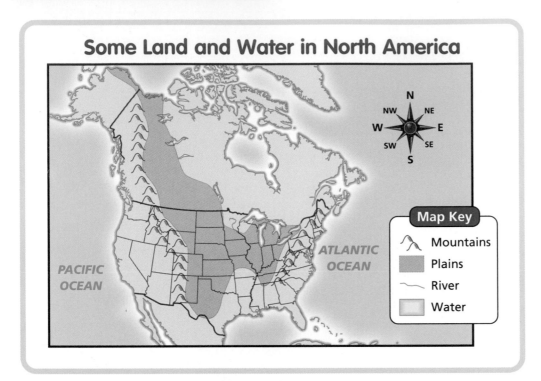

Some Land and Water in North America

ATLANTIC OCEAN

PACIFIC OCEAN

Map Key
- Mountains
- Plains
- River
- Water

What are the missing words?

1. The map shows part of the _____ of North America. 2. A body of water on this map is _____. 3. A landform shown is _____.

Facts and Main Ideas

4. Which kind of landform has water all around it? (page 76)

5. How are weather and climate related? (pages 84, 85)

6. Describe two types of regions. (page 92)

7. Name a natural resource that can be replaced. (page 102)

Vocabulary

Choose the missing word in each sentence.

8. A _____ is low land between hills or mountains.

9. A nation may also be called a _____.

10. The _____ is the natural world around us.

11. A landform that has water on three sides is a _____.

A. **country** (page 67)

B. **region** (page 92)

C. **valley** (page 75)

D. **peninsula** (page 76)

E. **environment** (page 103)

✔ Test Practice

12. What do the words **natural resource** mean?

    A. something that people make

    B. something in nature that people use

    C. a place where people cannot live

    D. something that can never be replaced

Critical Thinking

Compare and Contrast

13. Describe a way that people have harmed the environment.

14. Describe a way that people have cared for the environment.

Skillbuilders Parts of a Globe

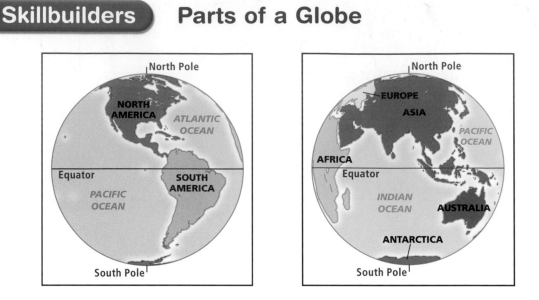

15. What are two bodies of water on the globe?

16. Which two continents are completely in the Southern Hemisphere?

17. On a globe, the equator passes through three continents. Which three are they?

Use Intermediate Directions

18. In which direction do you go to get from Phoenix, Arizona, to Carson City, Nevada?

19. If you go southeast from Salt Lake City, which city do you reach first?

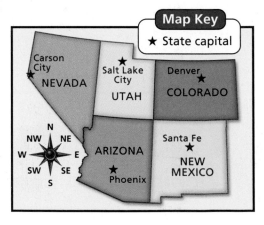

Unit Activity

Keep a Weather Log

Keep track of the weather for a week. Use that information to make a weather log.

❶ Record the temperature each day.

❷ Note whether it is cloudy, sunny, raining, or snowing.

❸ Make a weather map for one day to go with your log.

CURRENT EVENTS
WEEKLY (WR) READER

Current Events Project

Make a 3-D landform map. Find information about places from the Weekly Reader at the Social Studies Website.

The Sierra Nevada Mountains

Technology

Current Events Project
For current events information, go to:
www.eduplace.com/kids/hmss05/

In Your Classroom

Look for these Social Studies Independent Books in your classroom.

At the Library

You may find these books at your school or public library.

Mountains

By Claire Llewellyn

Hottest, Coldest, Highest, Deepest

By Steve Jenkins

UNIT 3

Ways of Living

66 The world's a lovely
Place to be
Because we are
A family. 99
—Mary Ann Hoberman, Poet

The Big Idea

What are some of the cultures that make up your community, state, and nation?

Vocabulary Preview

Technology

e • **glossary**
e • **word games**
www.eduplace.com/kids/hmss05/

culture

Culture is the way of life of a group of people. Stories are a part of culture. page 117

tradition

A **tradition,** such as Thanksgiving, is something that people do the same way year after year. page 126

Reading Strategy

Use the **summarize** reading strategy in Lessons 1 and 2 and the **predict and infer** strategy in Lessons 3 and 4.

memorial

A **memorial** honors a hero or an event. The Crazy Horse Memorial honors a chief of the Lakota people. page 140

landmark

The Golden Gate Bridge is a San Francisco landmark. A **landmark** is something that helps people know a place. page 138

Families from Many Places

Vocabulary

custom
culture
immigrant
ancestor

Reading Skill

Draw Conclusions

Build on What You Know

What are some special times when your family meets with other families or with relatives?

Family Customs

A **custom** is something that people usually do at a certain time. Most families have customs. Look at examples on these pages.

main idea (★)

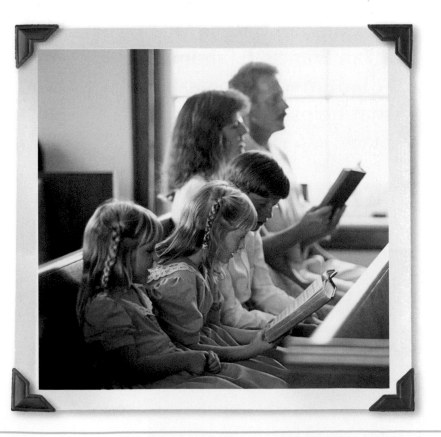

Mary's family sings in church on Sundays.

Families and Cultures

Culture is the way of life of a group of people. The clothes you wear and the foods you eat are part of your culture. Music and language are part of culture. Your religion and your customs are part of your culture too. <u>You learn about your culture from your family, by doing things and by talking together.</u> (★ main idea)

Carla's grandma always makes a piñata for her birthday.

Review What is a custom that is part of a culture you know?

Many Cultures in One Country

The United States has many different cultures. Some cultures come from American Indian groups. Some cultures come from immigrant groups. **Immigrants** are people who move from one country to live in another. Many immigrants have come to the United States for freedom. Immigrants from many countries have brought their ways of living to the United States.

Havre

San Francisco

New York City

A Chinese New Year's Day parade in San Francisco.

Many American Indian groups celebrate their cultures in powwows like this one in Havre, Montana.

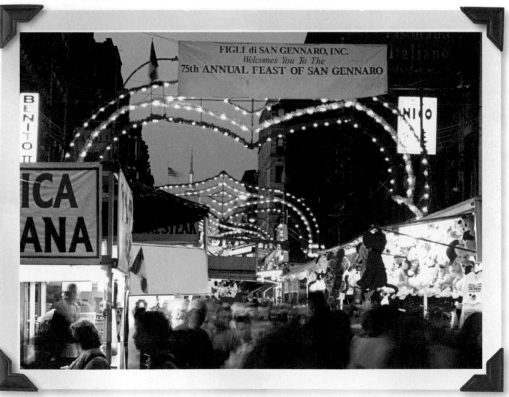

Immigrants from Italy brought customs such as this street fair in New York City.

Review What are two celebrations that came from immigrant groups?

Cultures from Ancestors

An **ancestor** is someone in your family who lived before you were born. You can learn about your culture by learning about your ancestors. You can learn from old pictures of them. You can also look at things that once belonged to them. Even your name can tell about your ancestors and their cultures. One family can have more than one culture.

My first name, Kumar, comes from India, where my mother was born. My last name, Bloomstein, comes from Russia, where my father's grandparents were born.

My first name is Isabel, from my mama's Latina family from Ecuador. My middle name is Taysin, from my mama's Chinese culture. My last name is Carter, from my father's ancestors in England.

Review What is one way that children can learn about their ancestors?

Lesson Review

❶ **Vocabulary** Tell something about the United States using the words **immigrant** and **ancestor.**

❷ **Main Idea** Does the United States have only one culture? Tell why you answered yes or no.

Activity Write or tell about a custom in your family. Tell when, where, and why your family does it.

Immigrants at Ellis Island

A boy named Yehuda (yeh HOO duh) came to America from Russia in 1922. Visit Ellis Island with him.

Yehuda saw a man approaching with a big bucket filled with milk and a basket of long yellow fruit. He was stopping at every child, giving each one a cup of milk and one of the strange pieces of fruit. Yehuda watched as one boy bit right into the yellow skin, made a face, and spit it out. Then he saw someone pull the skin down in strips and eat the soft, white fruit inside. Yehuda smiled to himself—every day in America he was learning something new!

Women and children at Ellis Island getting snacks

Activities

1. **Act It Out** Role-play the story about getting fruit and milk.

2. **Write About It** Describe the face, hair, and clothes of a person in the picture.

Read a Timeline

▶ **Vocabulary**

timeline

Every family has a history. A timeline can show events in a family's history. A **timeline** is an ordered group of words and dates that shows when events happened.

Look at the timeline of Andrea's family.

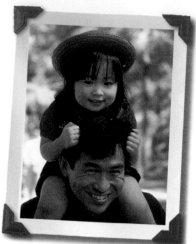

Learn the Skill

Step 1 The title tells what the timeline is about. The timeline has a line divided in equal parts. Each part stands for 10 years.

Step 2 Look at the first and last numbers on the timeline. The numbers are years. The events on the timeline happened between these years.

Step 3 The numbers with the events on the timeline tell the year in which each event happened.

1930	1940	1950

1946
Andrea's grand-father is born.

1935
Andrea's great-grandmother comes to the United States from Japan.

Use the timeline to answer the questions below.

1 Was Andrea's grandfather born before, or after, her great-grandmother came to the United States?

2 When did Andrea's great-grandmother come to the United States?

3 What happened in 1994?

Andrea's Family History

1960   1970   1980   1990   2000

1970
Andrea's father is born.

1965
Andrea's grandparents marry.

1994
Andrea's parents marry.

1999
Andrea is born.

Sharing Cultures

Vocabulary

tradition
legend

Reading Skill

Main Idea and Details

Build on What You Know

Have you sung songs with words in another language? When people share songs of different languages, they share cultures.

Traditions from Cultures

A **tradition** is something that people do the same way year after year. It might be a special holiday meal or clothes for an event. Often families keep a tradition that comes from the culture of their ancestors. Families share their cultures by sharing their traditions with others.

main idea

Sharing Traditions

Izumi's (ih ZOO mihz) grandmother learned origami, a paper-folding tradition, from her parents in Japan. She taught it to Izumi. Together they taught origami to other children in Izumi's class.

Review What traditions do you follow in your family?

Sharing Stories and Art

Every culture has stories. People share their cultures by sharing stories called legends. A **legend** is a story that people have passed along for years and years. Many legends come from a time when people told stories but did not write them. Later, people wrote them in books.

"The Fox and the Crab" is a legend from China. It is in a book of legends from many different countries.

Art is another way of sharing cultures. People can see art in many different places.

main idea (★)

Review What are two ways of sharing culture?

Thomas Hart Benton was famous for painting scenes from the Midwest, such as this painting called "The Boy."

Indians of the Pacific coast carved beautiful totem poles like this.

Artists Who Teach

Some artists share their culture by teaching. Alan Hezekiah (hehz ih KEYE uh) is a musician who teaches drumming to children and adults. Alicia Adame-Molinar (ah LEE see uh ad DAHM ay MOH lee nahr) teaches Mexican dances.

"Drums are in every culture, all around the world. I always wanted to be a drummer. I chose to play drums from Africa because I am an African American. When I play my drum I feel that I am connecting across the oceans, across the years!"

"I was born in Mexico, where music and dancing are very important. I learned many dances when I was growing up. Now I want to share my culture with people in this country. They can learn so much about Mexico when they learn the music and dances!"

Review What is one way that the drummer and dancer on these pages are alike?

Lesson Review

1 **Vocabulary** Write or tell an example of a **legend** and an example of a **tradition.**

2 **Main Idea** How can one family learn about another family's culture?

Activity Draw a picture of someone who has shared his or her culture with you. Tell about your picture.

Yo-Yo Ma

Yo-Yo Ma was only four years old when he learned to play a cello (CHEHL oh). While still a boy, Yo-Yo Ma moved with his family from France to the United States. He kept studying the cello. His music amazed people.

Yo-Yo Ma plays with musicians from other cultures. He believes that music helps people from all cultures understand one another.

Sharing Musical Traditions

As a grownup, Yo-Yo Ma has become a famous musician. He has played concerts around the world. He is excited about music from many cultures. In 1998, he started bringing together musicians from many cultures. They share their musical traditions. They learn from one another and make new music too.

Today Yo-Yo Ma is a U.S. citizen.

Activities

1. **Discuss It** Why does Yo-Yo Ma want musicians to share traditions?

2. **Write About It** Write or tell two things you learned about Yo-Yo Ma.

Technology More biographies at www.eduplace.com/kids/hmss05/

Conduct an Interview

▶ **Vocabulary**

interview

In an **interview,** a reporter asks a person questions about a topic.

Learn the Skill

Think of someone you know in your community. What would you like to know about that person's past or traditions?

Step 1 Prepare your interview questions. Write four or five questions you can ask. Good questions start with words like **who, what, where, when, how, why,** and **what kind of.** . . .

Step 2 Practice asking your interview questions. Ask one question at a time.

Step 3 You may want to rewrite some of your questions.

Practice the Skill

Set up a time to do your interview. Then follow the directions.

1 Think about what you want to know. Write your questions. Decide the order in which you wish to ask them.

2 Bring a notebook and pencil so that you can take notes. If possible, bring a tape recorder.

3 Be polite. Listen carefully to each answer. Thank the person when you are finished.

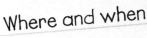

Where and when were you born?

What did you like to do when you were young?

How did your family celebrate traditional ways?

What kind of stories did your family tell?

Hints for Tape Recording

Make sure your tape recorder is working and has a tape. Ask whether you can tape record the conversation.

America's Symbols

Vocabulary

symbol
landmark
President
monument
memorial

Reading Skill
Classify

Build on What You Know What would you put in a picture to stand for the United States? Pictures, buildings, and statues can stand for a country.

Culture and Symbols

In the United States, people have traditions that have come from many cultures. They also share traditions that began in this country. The United States has a culture from those traditions.

What are some symbols in the seal of the President of the United States?

A **symbol** is a picture, place, or thing that stands for something else. For example, a picture of a bicycle may be a symbol for a bike path.

Symbols for the United States remind people that they are part of one country. The American flag is the symbol people use most often for the United States.

main idea (★)

Review Why are symbols for the United States important to people who live here?

Uncle Sam

American Landmarks

A **landmark** is something that helps people know a place. A sign or statue may be a landmark. <u>Many landmarks are symbols for America.</u> Look at some on these pages. The map shows where they are.

main idea ★

Mount Rushmore
Black Hills, South Dakota

The leader of the United States of America is called the **President.** An artist and many helpers carved the faces of four important Presidents in the stone of this mountain. The faces are 60 feet high!

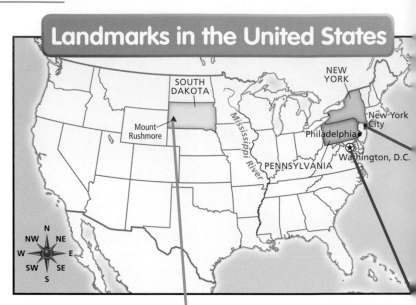

Landmarks in the United States

George Washington

Thomas Jefferson

Theodore Roosevelt

Abraham Lincoln

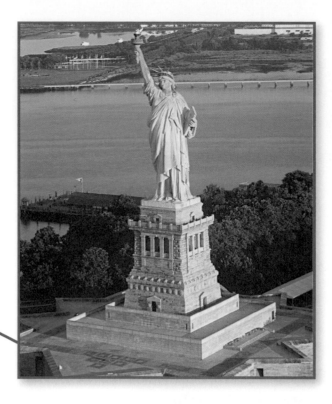

Statue of Liberty
New York Bay, New York

This statue is the size of a tall building. A French artist sent the great statue as a gift from his country more than a hundred years ago. The statue still welcomes immigrants and visitors to America.

Liberty Bell
Philadelphia, Pennsylvania

Americans rang this bell at the start of their new country in 1776. You can still visit it in Philadelphia. Pictures of the Liberty Bell are symbols for freedom in America.

Review Why is the Statue of Liberty an important landmark?

Monuments and Memorials

Many buildings and statues honor heroes or events. Some are called **monuments.** Others are called **memorials.** Both can be landmarks. Monuments and memorials help people remember. These monuments and memorials are in Washington, D.C.

main idea (★)

Lincoln Memorial

Abraham Lincoln was the President of the United States during the Civil War. Two of his best known speeches are printed on the walls of the memorial.

Washington Monument

The Washington Monument honors George Washington. He was the first President of the United States. He was known for being brave, strong, and honest.

Thomas Jefferson Memorial

Thomas Jefferson was the third President. He wrote the Declaration of Independence. That was the paper that said that the United States should have freedom from Great Britain. Some of his words are printed on the walls of the memorial.

Review Why do people build monuments and memorials to Presidents?

Lesson Review

1 **Vocabulary** Tell what is the same about monuments and memorials.

2 **Main Idea** What are some symbols that remind us that we are all members of one country?

HANDS ON **Activity** Draw one of the symbols of the United States. Tell what you think and feel about the symbol.

The Star-Spangled Banner

The year was 1814. The United States was at war. All night Francis Scott Key watched the British fire cannons at an American fort. Its flag stayed up during the battle. This proved to Key that the United States was strong. He was so proud, he wrote a poem.

The poem that Key wrote was set to music. It became the anthem of the United States. An anthem is a song that is a **symbol** of a place.

Fort McHenry in Baltimore, Maryland

The Star-Spangled Banner

Oh, say can you see, by the dawn's early
    light,

What so proudly we hailed at the twilight's
    last gleaming?

Whose broad stripes and bright stars,
    through the perilous fight,

O'er the ramparts we watched, were so
    gallantly streaming?

And the rockets' red glare, the bombs
    bursting in air,

Gave proof through the night that
    our flag was still there.

O say, does that star-spangled
    banner yet wave

O'er the land of the free and the
    home of the brave?

Activities

1. **Talk About It** Explain how a song can be a
   symbol of a country.

2. **Write About It** Choose a line of words in the
   song and tell what you think the words mean.

We Celebrate Holidays

Vocabulary
national holiday
religious holiday

Reading Skill
Classify

Build on What You Know Name some holidays you celebrate. Find out how holidays are alike and different.

National Holidays

A holiday is a day that honors a person or an event. A **national holiday** honors someone or something that is important to the country. The date for a national holiday is the same everywhere in the country. Schools and many workplaces are closed so that families and friends can celebrate together.

main idea

Presidents' Day is a national holiday that honors two American Presidents, George Washington and Abraham Lincoln.

State Holidays

Some holidays are state holidays. A state holiday usually honors an event or a person who is important to that state. Schools and workplaces may be closed, but only in the state where people celebrate that holiday. In California, for example, people celebrate Cesar Chavez Day of Service and Learning.

Review What is a way that state holidays are different from national holidays?

Massachusetts and Maine celebrate Patriots' Day. It honors events that took place in those states during the American Revolution.

Religious Holidays

People who belong to a religion share a set of beliefs about God. They may have times each year to honor events that go with the beliefs of their religion. These times are called **religious holidays.**

main idea

Ramadan
For the month of Ramadan, Muslims do not eat or drink during the day. They say prayers at certain times. After sunset, people eat and visit with one another.

Easter
For Easter, Christians say special prayers in church. Some Christians give up certain foods for a time before Easter. Eggs and flowers are symbols of the holiday.

Passover
For Passover, Jews have a meal called a seder, with prayers, songs, and symbols. For about a week, Jews do not eat most kinds of bread, cakes, or cookies.

Review What are some things people do on religious holidays?

Other Holidays

Some holidays are not religious, state, or national holidays. Some holidays honor traditions of a culture.

A Saint Patrick's Day parade

Lesson Review

1 **Vocabulary** Write a sentence about a **religious holiday** and a sentence about a **national holiday.**

2 **Main Idea** Explain how a national holiday is different from a religious holiday.

HANDS ON **Activity** Draw a picture of people celebrating a holiday you like. Tell if it is a national, state, or religious holiday.

Cesar Chavez

When Cesar Chavez was ten, his life changed for the worse. His family lost their home and became farm workers. Both grownups and children worked very hard in fields for very low pay. Often they were treated unfairly.

Cesar Chavez wanted to change how farm workers were treated. As a grownup in California, he led farm workers in their struggle for better pay and safety. Chavez was a strong, caring leader. He often said, "¡Si se puede!" (see say PWAY day). It means "Yes we can!" People believed in him. In California many schools do service projects on the state holiday that honors him.

Activities

1. **Discuss It** What did Chavez do to help make things more fair?

2. **Write About It** Write or tell about a service project children could do or have done in your school.

Technology Read more biographies at www.eduplace.com/kids/hmss05/

Make a Decision

▶ **Vocabulary**

decision

Good citizens think before they make decisions. To make a **decision,** you make up your mind. It may help to compare choices in a chart.

Learn the Skill

Suppose that your class wants to do a project that helps the school. Many children like two different ideas. How do you make a decision?

Step 1 Put the ideas in a chart that shows what is good and not good about each choice. Use plus (+) for good and minus (-) for not good. Look at the example on this page.

Step 2 Think and talk about what is good and not good about each choice. Write your thoughts in the chart.

Step 3 Compare choices in the chart. You might ask: Which choice will help more people in the school? Decide which choice is better.

School Clean-up Day	School Garden
+ School will look better. More school pride	**+** Beautiful flowers Healthful vegetables
− Hard work Not fun	**−** Takes too long. Might not grow.

Practice the Skill

Follow the directions to help Nino make a decision.

1 Look at the pictures and read the words. Tell what Nino's choices are.

2 Make a chart to show what is good about each choice and what is not good about each choice.

3 Think of a question Nino might ask to help him decide. Use the question and the chart to make a choice.

Big Ideas

The Big Idea

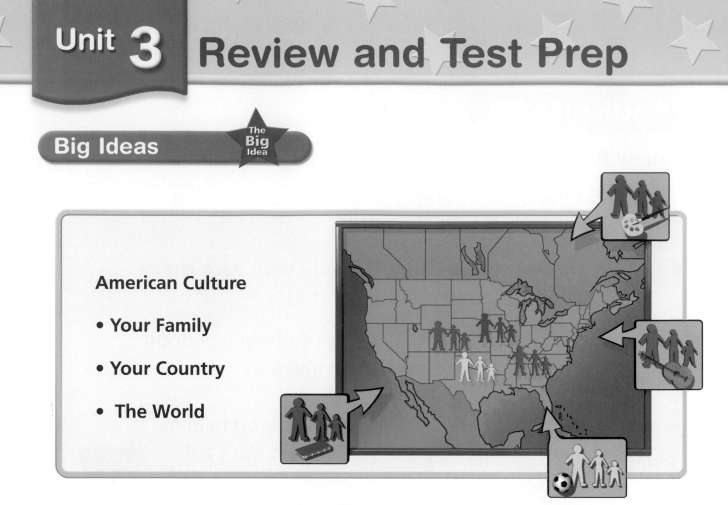

American Culture

• **Your Family**

• **Your Country**

• **The World**

Choose words that help describe the picture.

Your culture comes from your **1.** _____ and your **2.** _____.
Languages and traditions are part of **3.** _____ .

Facts and Main Ideas

4. In what way do immigrants change American culture?
   (pages 118, 119)

5. What are two languages that people might speak in the
   United States? (pages 118–121)

6. Who has been honored by an American monument or
   memorial? (pages 138, 140–141)

7. What are two symbols of the United States? (page 139)

8. What is one tradition that is part of a religious holiday? (page 146)

Vocabulary

Choose the letter of the word to match the correct sentence.

9. A story that has been passed along for a long time

10. Something that people keep doing in the same way

11. A person who lived before us

12. A building or monument that helps people know a place

A. **ancestor** (page 120)

B. **landmark** (page 138)

C. **legend** (page 128)

D. **immigrant** (page 118)

E. **tradition** (page 126)

Test Practice

13. What do the words **national holiday** mean?

    A. a special day for people of a religion

    B. a day when events or people important to a state are honored

    C. a day when events or people important to a nation are honored

    D. a building that honors a famous person

Critical Thinking

Classify

14. Name a state holiday and tell why people celebrate it.

Skillbuilders   **Read a Timeline**

Dan's Life History

| 0 | 1 | 2 | 3 | 4 | 5 | 6 | 7 | 8 | 9 |

Dan was born   **Dan learned to read**   **Dan today**

15. How old is Dan today?

16. What did Dan do when he was six?

Make a Decision

17. What can Nora do? Name two or three choices.

18. Make a chart for each choice to show what is good or bad about it.

Good	Bad

19. What should Nora choose? Tell reasons for your decision.

Unit Activity

Culture Banner

Use pictures to make an American culture banner that shows the many people and symbols that make up our country's culture.

❶ Draw or bring in pictures to put on the banner.

❷ Write a title and your name on a banner.

❸ Arrange the pictures on your banner.

Current Events Project

Make an exhibit about celebrations in the news. Use information from the Weekly Reader at the Social Studies Website.

Technology

Current Events Project
For current events information, go to
www.eduplace.com/kids/hmss05/

In Your Classroom

Look for these Social Studies Independent Books in your classroom.

At the Library

You may find these books at your school or public library.

Grandma Maxine Remembers
by Ann Morris

Everybody Brings Noodles
by Norah Dooley

UNIT 4

People at Work

"At Dudley Market
now I tell
Most kinds of articles
they sell:
Hats, caps and bonnets blue
And trousers wide
enough for two"

—Ben Boucher, Poet

The Big Idea

What are ways
people earn, spend,
and save money?

Vocabulary Prevew

Technology

e • **glossary**
e • **word games**
www.eduplace.com/kids/hmss05/

consumer

A **consumer** is someone who buys goods or services. You are a consumer when you buy crayons. page 166

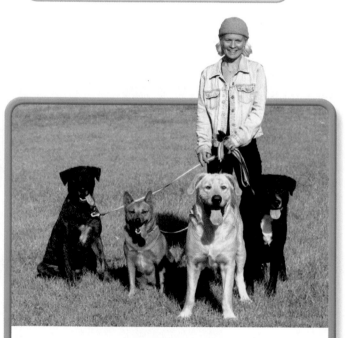

producer

A **producer** is someone who provides a service or makes goods. Julie has a dogwalking service, so she is a producer. page 166

Reading Strategy

Use the **question** reading strategy in Lessons 1, 2, and 3 and the **summarize** strategy in Lessons 4, 5, and 6.

income

The money people earn when they work is their **income.** Sam's income is the $5.00 he earns each week on his paper route.

page 168

price

Price is the amount of money you pay to buy something. If you look in two or three stores, you may find the same toy at different prices. page 180

Write On!

Fancy Pencils with erasers
30¢

ERASERS
10¢

BASIC PENCILS (without erasers)
15¢

Needs, Wants, and Choices

Vocabulary

needs

shelter

wants

Reading Skill

Predict Outcomes

Build on What You Know

Have you bought anything at a store? What choices did you make?

Needs and Wants

Needs are things that people must have to live. Everyone has to have food, water, clothing, and shelter. Shelter is something that protects or covers. Houses, trailer homes, and apartments are kinds of shelter.

Wants are things that people would like to have. People do not have to have those things to live. Everyone has wants and needs.

main idea

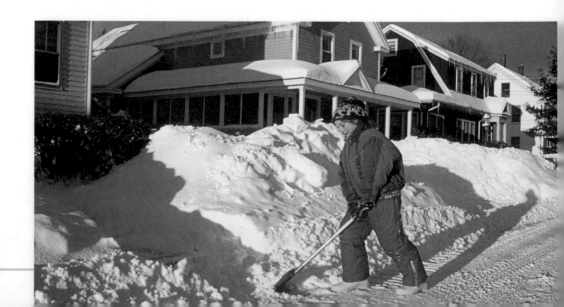

Making Choices

People cannot have everything they want. <u>People</u>
<u>have to make choices about what to buy.</u> If they use
all their money to buy one thing, they cannot buy
something else.

> I have $30 saved.
> I can buy a computer game and play
> with it today. Or I can buy a scooter
> and ride it in the spring.

Sally's Choices

Choices	What I Give Up	What I Get
Buy computer game	Ride scooter in spring	Enjoy computer game today
Buy scooter	Enjoy computer game today	Ride scooter in spring

Review If Sally buys the computer game, what
does she give up?

Lesson Review

❶ **Vocabulary** Name some **needs** and some **wants.**

❷ **Main Idea** Which would you choose, the game or
the scooter? Why?

▶ **Activity** List as many kinds of shelter as you can.

161

Literature

THE MILKMAID

"The Milkmaid" is a tale told in Mexico and many other countries.

❖ ❖ ❖

Maria was a milkmaid who worked for a rich family. Sometimes the family gave Maria their leftover milk. Maria made extra money by selling the milk. One day the family gave Maria enough milk to fill a big jug.

On her way to market to sell the milk she thought, "I will have money to buy a hen that will lay many eggs. I will sell the eggs and use the money to buy a pig."

"When the pig has grown large, I will sell it and buy a cow. My cow will always give me milk to sell."

Maria thought of all the money she would make, and skipped with joy. Then, oops! Down she fell! Crash went the milk jug! Out spilled the milk, and with it Maria's dreams.

Maria cried and cried. Finally she said, "I may not get all I wanted, but I still have what I need."

Activities

1. **Write About It** Make a list of all of Maria's wants.

2. **Think About It** When Maria says, "I still have what I need," what are some needs she may be thinking of?

163

Skillbuilder

Compare Fact and Fiction

▶ **Vocabulary**

fiction

nonfiction

fact

Fiction books are about made-up things. **Nonfiction** books tell facts. A **fact** is something that is true.

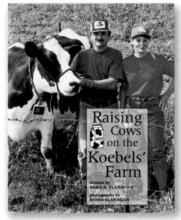

Learn the Skill

Step 1 Read the title. This title shows that the book is a true story about a real family farm.

Step 2 Look at the words and the pictures. The words in this book tell facts. The photographs show real things and people.

Step 3 Decide if the book is fiction, or nonfiction. Tell why you think so.

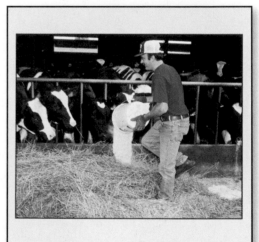

Mr. Koebel is in charge of the cows, or the herd. He is called the herdsman.

10

Practice the Skill

Follow the directions.

1 Look at the book titles below. Which book is fiction?

2 Look at the book pages. How can you tell that the fiction book is fiction?

Sheep graze on grass and other plants.

Sheep chomp. Sheep sneeze.

Ways to Earn Money

When people work, they usually earn money. This money is their **income.**

One person's income may be earned from selling a painting he made. Another person may earn money by selling a crop she grew. Sometimes people sell their skills or their time. They are paid for teaching in a school or working in a shop. People do different kinds of work.

main
(★)
idea

I own a small business. I like to help people with computer problems. I also like being my own boss!

I run this machine. I am really good at making cars.

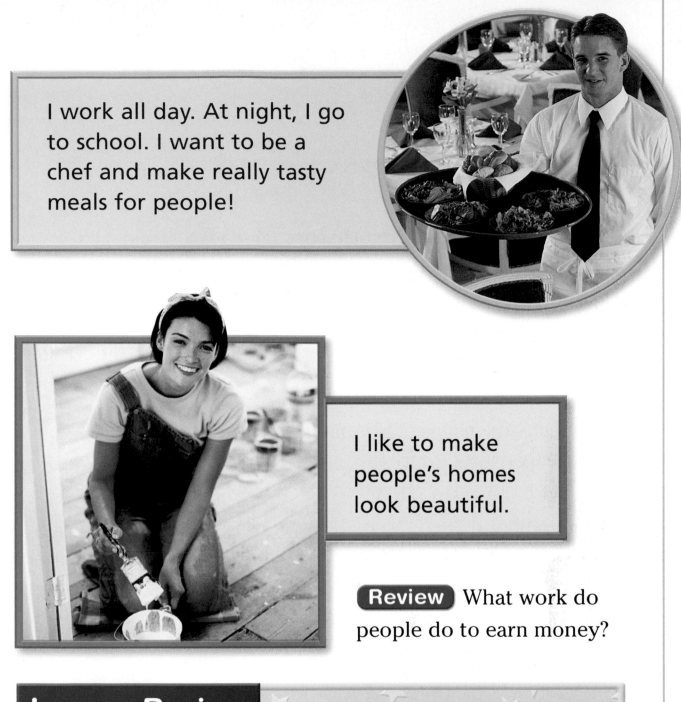

I work all day. At night, I go to school. I want to be a chef and make really tasty meals for people!

I like to make people's homes look beautiful.

Review What work do people do to earn money?

Lesson Review

 Vocabulary Name two ways to earn **income.**

 Main Idea What is a way that someone can be both a producer and a consumer?

HANDS ON **Activity** Draw a picture that shows a job you might like to do someday.

First Farmers

Were people always producers of their food? Look back more than ten thousand years. People did not have cities, towns, or farms. Instead, they moved from place to place. They gathered wild plants to eat.

Some of the first farmers lived in Mesopotamia.

Then some people took seeds from the strongest wild grains. They planted the seeds. The plants grew well. People picked the grain. They used some of it and saved the rest for planting.

2. Planting seeds

Having plants to care for, farmers began to live near their fields. Small towns grew up nearby.

1. Making tools

First farmers needed tools to plant seeds and cut grain.

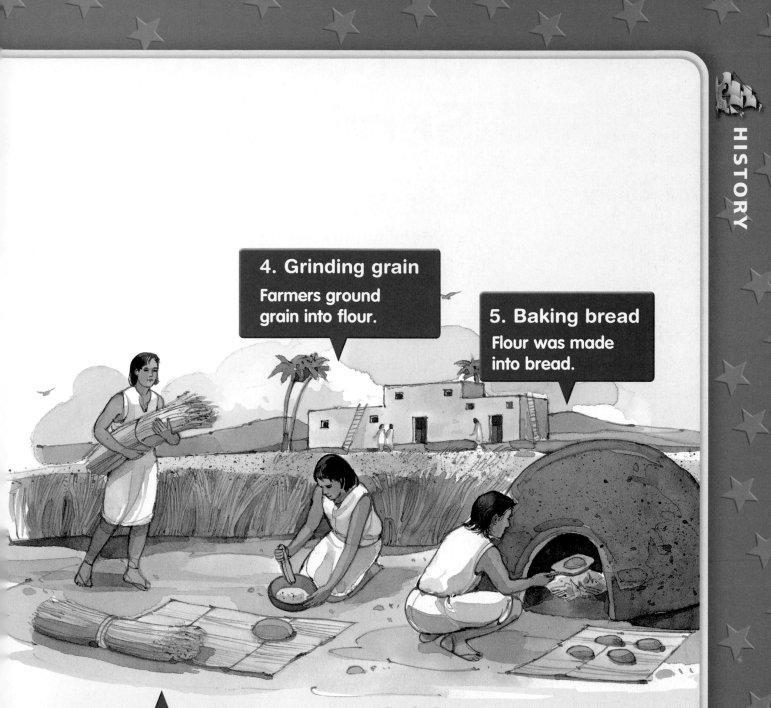

4. Grinding grain
Farmers ground grain into flour.

5. Baking bread
Flour was made into bread.

3. Harvesting grain
Farmers cut the grain. Some was stored away.

Activities

1. **Chart It** Make a flow chart showing the steps described in the words and pictures on these pages.

2. **Think About It** For thousands of years, people gathered wild grain. Why do you think people decided to grow it instead?

Goods and Services

Vocabulary

goods
factory
services

Reading Skill

Classify

Build on What You Know Have you ever wondered how your clothing was made or who made your toys?

Goods

The things people make or grow are called goods. **Goods** are things that you can touch, such as cars, apples, and baseballs. Many goods are made in a **factory**. A factory is a building where people work to make goods.

These people are working in a shoe factory.

Services

Some people are doctors, teachers, or dogwalkers. Those people do not make things. They provide **services**. Services are activities that people do to help other people.

Review What are some services that you use?

Lesson Review

1 **Vocabulary** What are some **goods** that you use?

2 **Main Idea** What is one way goods are different from services?

Activity Make a picture chart showing goods and services.

SCIENTISTS SERVING OTHERS

Some scientists discover things that help many people.

Marie Curie had a good memory that helped her as a student in Poland. When she grew up, she became a scientist. She lived and worked in France with her husband Pierre. Together, they made some big discoveries. Other scientists built on their work to find ways of curing sick people and making energy.

Louis Pasteur (LOO ee pas TUR) When Louis Pasteur was a boy, his teacher saw that Louis was patient and hardworking. Later, those qualities helped Pasteur become one of France's most famous scientists. He found that heating milk killed germs. That made the milk safer to drink. Pasteur's discoveries have helped millions of people stay healthy. Milk is still heated today. The process is called pasteurization. (pas chuhr ih ZAY shuhn)

George Washington Carver The plant scientist
George Washington Carver wanted to help African
American farmers make more money from the crops they
grew. After many experiments and much hard work,
Carver found hundreds of ways to use peanuts, soybeans,
and sweet potatoes. Then, he thought, farmers could earn
income by growing these plants too.

Eloy Rodriguez (ee LOY rahd REE gehs) Think on your feet. Use common sense. Eloy Rodriguez often heard that advice in Spanish from his family. Now he is a scientist who studies how animals use plants to heal themselves. From this he has learned ways that plants can heal people. Also Eloy Rodriguez gets students excited about science. He shares advice that helped him.

Activities

1. **Think About It** What are some ways these scientists show caring for others?

2. **Write About It** Write or tell how people's lives are better because of the work of the scientists you have read about.

Read a Bar Graph

Many foods are produced in the United States. This bar graph shows how much milk cows produce each year.

▶ **Vocabulary**

bar graph

Learn the Skill

Using a **bar graph** is a way to compare things. The bars show how much there is of something.

Step 1 The numbers and words at the side of the graph tell how much. On this graph, the number 30 stands for 30 billion pounds of milk.

Step 2 Along the bottom of the graph are the names of some states in which milk is produced.

Step 3 Look at the bar above California. It goes up to 30. That means that in California, cows produce 30 billion pounds of milk each year. How much milk do cows in Wisconsin produce?

Look at the graph below. Then answer the questions.

1 How much milk is produced in New York each year?

2 In which state on the graph is the smallest amount of milk produced?

3 In which state do cows produce more milk each year, Wisconsin or New York?

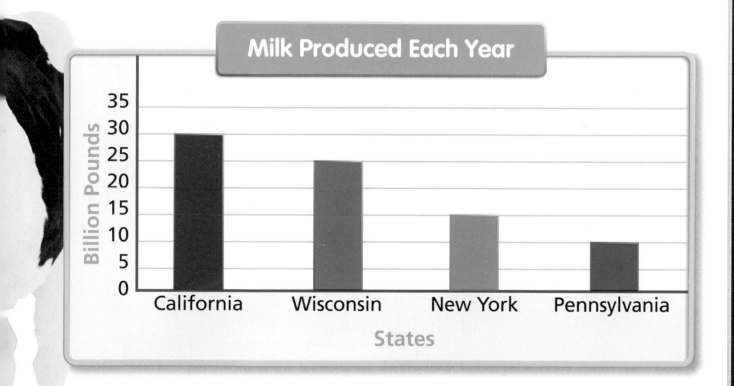

Milk Produced Each Year

People Save Money

Vocabulary
price
bank
savings account

Reading Skill
Predict Outcomes

Build on What You Know

Suppose you are given $2.00 for helping a neighbor. What will you do with it? Will you buy something now, or keep it for later?

Prices and Choices

The amount of money you pay to buy something is the **price.** In stores, often the prices are printed on or near things that people can buy. Looking at prices helps people decide what to buy. Ken has thirty cents to buy fruit today. The prices help him make his choice.

main idea (★)

What do you think Ken's choice will be? Why?

· 30¢ each

·40¢ each

·25¢ each

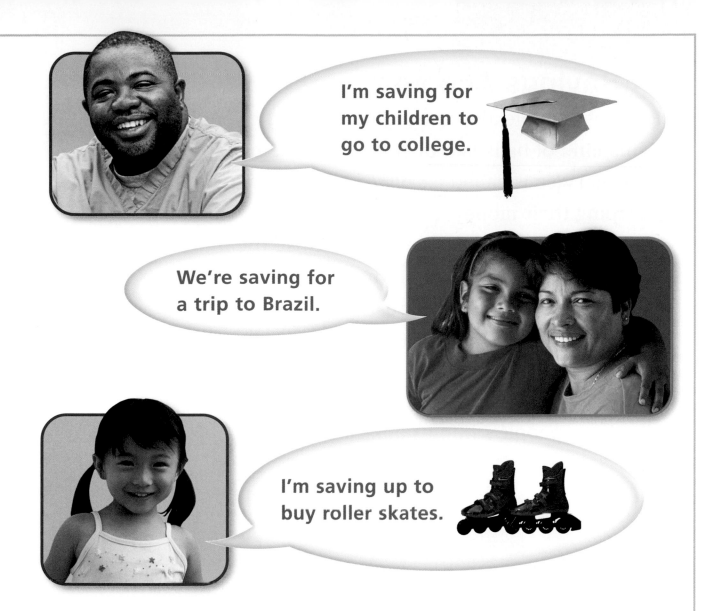

I'm saving for my children to go to college.

We're saving for a trip to Brazil.

I'm saving up to buy roller skates.

These people tell why they are saving money.

Saving Money

Many people are careful not to spend all their income. Some save money so they can pay for what they want. They save money in a bank. A **bank** is a safe place where people put in money or take it out.

main idea ⭐

Review Why do people save money?

A Savings Account

Most people also use a different kind of bank. This kind of bank is a business with many services. One service is called a **savings account.** Instead of keeping their money at home, people put it in a savings account. They let the bank use the money. In return, the bank adds a bit more money each month. That money is called interest. Interest helps the amount of money in the account grow faster.

main idea ★

Review How are banks that are businesses and banks in people's homes alike and different?

What services are in a bank?

Gina Saves

Gina has a savings account at a bank in her town. Last year she put in money every month to save for baseball camp in July. Look at the graph of Gina's account.

Money in Gina's Savings Account

Dollars

Months

April   May   June   July

Skill **Reading Graphs** What do you think Gina did with her money in July?

Lesson Review

❶ **Vocabulary** Describe a **savings account** in a bank.

❷ **Main Idea** What is one reason for saving money in banks that are businesses?

➤ **Activity** Write or tell about a buying choice you have made.

Spend Your Dollar

Welcome to Write On store. Take a look at what is for sale. Compare **prices.** Then see what your dollar will buy.

1. Look at the items. Choose the items you like.

2. You have only $1.00 to spend. Check the prices. See what you can buy with your $1.00.

3. Record on a class chart the items you choose. Add the prices and record the total.

Name	30¢	15¢	10¢	Total Spent
Frank	3	0	1	$1.00
Mimi	1	4	1	$1.00
George	2	2	1	$1.00
Amina	0	4	2	$0.80

Use Reference Books

You can find out more about a topic by using reference books.

► **Vocabulary**

dictionary
encyclopedia

Learn the Skill

A **dictionary** is a book that tells what words mean. An **encyclopedia** is a set of books that has articles on different topics. The articles tell facts.

Step 1 The information in reference books is often in ABC order. To find the word **bank** in a dictionary, look in the section that begins with B. To find an article about **banks** in an encyclopedia, look in the book labeled with the letter B.

Step 2 After you find the B section, you need to find the right page. The **guidewords** can help you. They show the first and last word on each page.

Step 3 Use ABC order to find the word **bank.**

Practice the Skill

Follow the directions.

1 Suppose your teacher asks you to find information about the first factories. Tell which kind of reference book you will use.

2 Use a dictionary to find the definition of these words: **product, income, business**

Guidewords

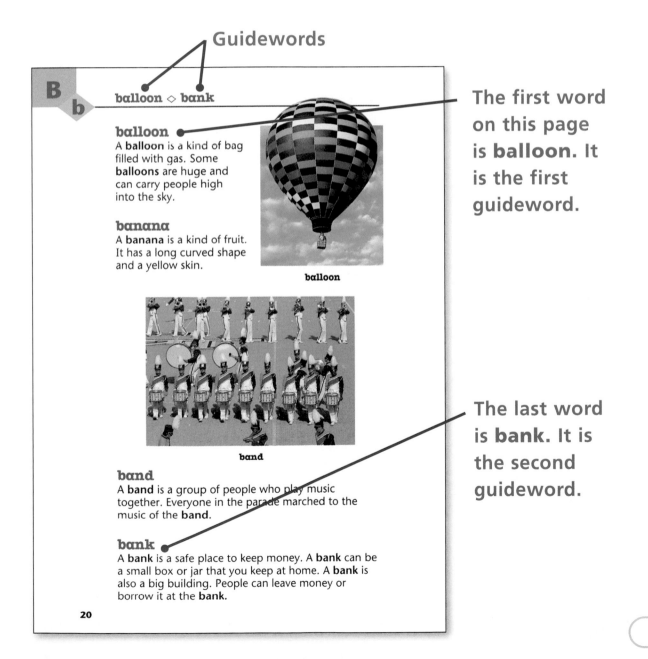

B b

balloon ◇ bank

balloon
A **balloon** is a kind of bag filled with gas. Some **balloons** are huge and can carry people high into the sky.

banana
A **banana** is a kind of fruit. It has a long curved shape and a yellow skin.

balloon

band

band
A **band** is a group of people who play music together. Everyone in the parade marched to the music of the **band**.

bank
A **bank** is a safe place to keep money. A **bank** can be a small box or jar that you keep at home. A **bank** is also a big building. People can leave money or borrow it at the **bank**.

20

The first word on this page is **balloon**. It is the first guideword.

The last word is **bank**. It is the second guideword.

From Field to Market

▶ **Vocabulary**
human resource
capital resource
scarcity

◎ **Reading Skill**
Sequence

Build on What You Know Do you know how a bunch of grapes becomes the box of raisins in your lunch?

From the Vine to You!

Imagine large farms with row after row of grapevines. In spring, workers start watering the vines. A few months later, the grapes are ripe. Workers pick the grape bunches by hand and place them on clean paper trays. The grapes dry in the sun for two to three weeks. Slowly they become raisins.

Picking grapes

Drying grapes

Workers drive the raisins to the food processing plant. There the raisins are checked and cleaned. Machines take off the stems and package the raisins. Ships, trains, and trucks carry the packages across the country and around the world. Stores sell the raisins to you! It takes many steps to get a box of raisins from a bunch of grapes.

main idea (★)

Review When do grapes become raisins?

Cleaning raisins   **Sorting raisins**   **Boxing raisins**

Three Kinds of Resources

Raisin producers use natural resources. They need soil, water, and sunshine. Raisin producers also need **human resources.** Human resources are people. They are the farm workers who care for the vines. They are the people who operate machines, sell raisins, and run the business.

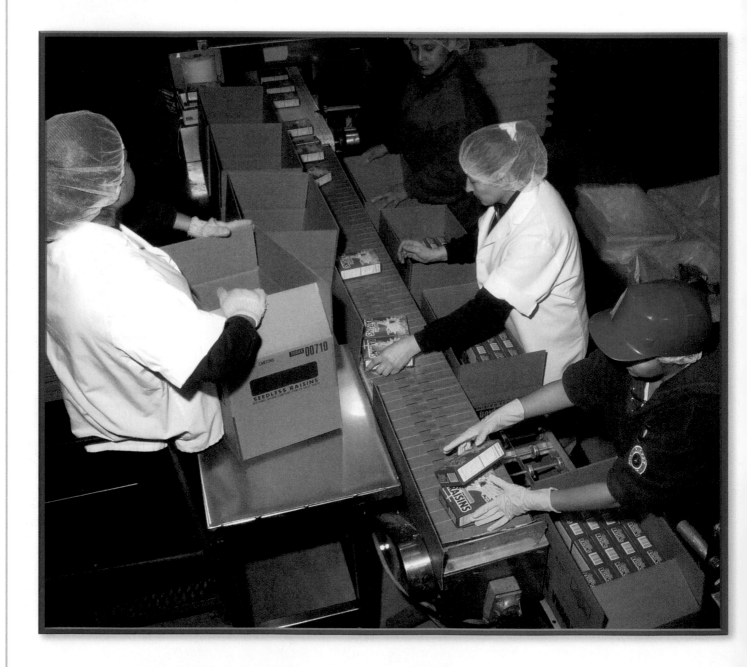

Raisin producers need a third kind of resource. They need capital resources. **Capital resources** are things such as tools, machinery, buildings, and trucks. The buildings where raisins are sorted and cleaned are capital resources. So are the machines that take the stems off the raisins. Producers of raisins and other goods use all three kinds of resources.

(★) main idea

Resources

Human Resources	Natural Resources	Capital Resources
farm workers sales people machine operators	soil water	machines trucks tools

Scarcity

The three kinds of resources are all limited. The earth has only so many human, natural, and capital resources. However, people have unlimited wants for goods and services. That is why there is scarcity.

Some farmers choose to use their land to grow grapes.

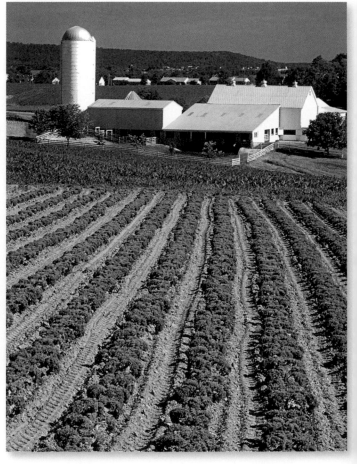

Some farmers choose to use their land for growing vegetables.

Scarcity means we don't have enough resources to produce all the goods and services we want. Because we can't have all we want, we have to make choices in what to make or grow.

Review Why do people have to make choices about what to make or grow?

Lesson Review

1 Vocabulary Explain what **scarcity** is.

2 Main Idea What are the three kinds of resources people use to produce goods and services?

 Activity List one example of each kind of resource in your school.

Keeping Food Cold

A Cool Timeline

For hundreds of years, people have found ways to keep food from spoiling by keeping it cold. There were many ways to keep food cold before people used refrigerators. Look at how the ways have changed.

1750   1800

250 years ago
Settlers dug root cellars inside or outside their homes.

1850	1900	1950	2000

170 years ago

A big block of ice kept food inside the ice box cold. The iceman delivered a new block of ice every other day or so.

80 to 90 years ago

People began using electric refrigerators with freezers.

Activities

1. **Talk About It** Tell a story about a time when the electricity was out and your family could not keep food cold in the refrigerator.

2. **Think About It** Why do you think a refrigerator is better than an ice box?

People and Nations Trade

Build on What You Know

Swapping toys or baseball cards with a friend is one way to get the things you want. What are other ways?

Barter

What you do when you swap toys or cards is called barter. **Barter** takes place when people exchange goods or services without using money. Long ago barter was the main way people got the things they wanted.

main idea

I'll give you this pig for two pounds of beets.

I'll trade one pound of beets for your pig.

Skill **Visual Learning** What do people use to help them trade goods?

Trade

Many times, barter does not work very well. That is why most people today pay for goods and services in other ways, often with money. Whether people barter or use money, they are taking part in trade. **Trade** is the buying and selling of goods and services. You take part in trade when you buy an apple.

Review What is one way you take part in trade?

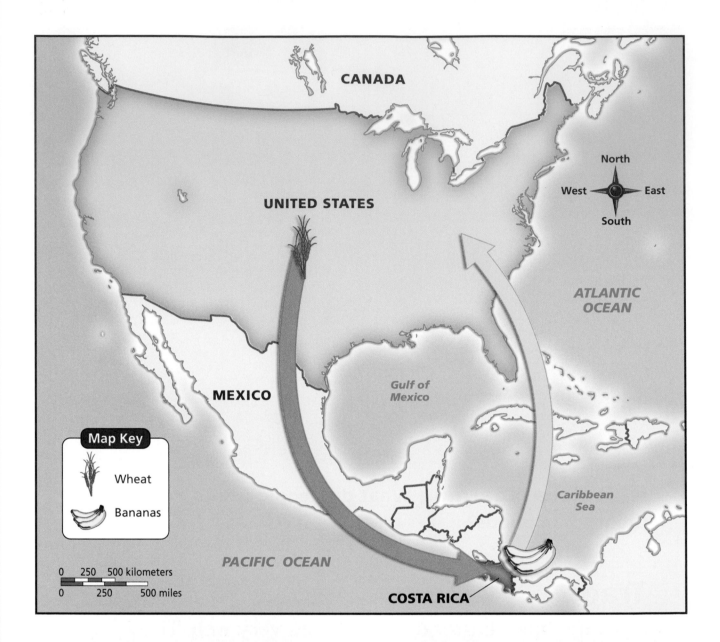

CANADA

UNITED STATES

North

West ✦ East

South

ATLANTIC
OCEAN

MEXICO

Gulf of
Mexico

Map Key

Wheat

Bananas

Caribbean
Sea

PACIFIC OCEAN

0   250   500 kilometers

0   250   500 miles

COSTA RICA

bananas

wheat

Depending on One Another

Farmers in the United States specialize in growing wheat, not bananas. Farmers in Costa Rica specialize in growing bananas, not wheat. When farmers **specialize,** that means they choose to grow mainly one crop. Farmers in the United States sell their wheat to consumers in Costa Rica. Farmers in Costa Rica sell their bananas to consumers in the United States. People in countries around the world depend on trade to get the goods and services they want.

Review What does it mean to specialize?

Lesson Review

❶ **Vocabulary** The buying and selling of goods and services is called _____.

❷ **Main Idea** What is one reason that countries trade with one another?

HANDS ON

Activity Draw a picture of something you want. Tell what you would be willing to barter to get it.

Money Around the World

There is an old saying that money cannot buy happiness. That's true, but money does buy a lot of other things. People everywhere use metal coins and paper bills to buy goods and services.

Countries around the world have their own money. The United States has the dollar. Jordan has the dinar. Find other money names.

The European Union

euro

euro cent

Brazil

real

centavo

Kenya

shilling

cent

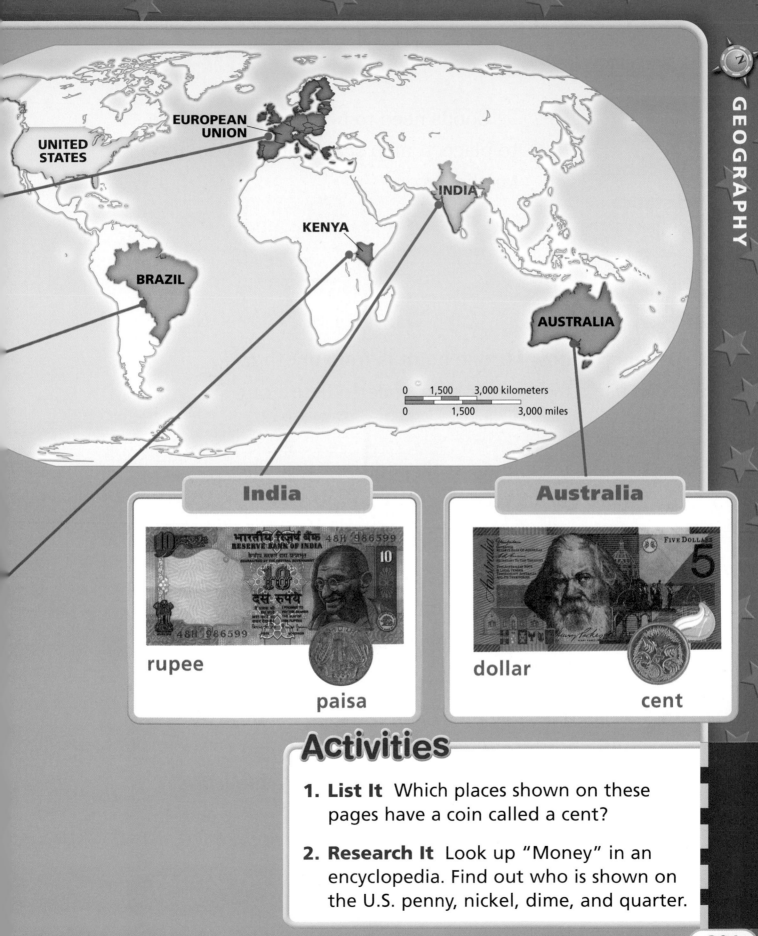

UNITED STATES

EUROPEAN UNION

INDIA

KENYA

BRAZIL

AUSTRALIA

0   1,500   3,000 kilometers

0   1,500   3,000 miles

India

rupee

paisa

Australia

dollar

cent

Activities

1. **List It** Which places shown on these pages have a coin called a cent?

2. **Research It** Look up "Money" in an encyclopedia. Find out who is shown on the U.S. penny, nickel, dime, and quarter.

Use a Map Scale

Goods need to be moved from place to place. A map scale can tell you how far they go.

▶ **Vocabulary**

distance

scale

Learn the Skill

Distance is how far one point is from another. You can use a map and a map **scale** to figure out distance.

Step 1 Look at the map scale and the ruler. The dark bar between 0 and 1 measures one inch.

Step 2 Look at the numbers on the scale. They show that one inch on the map stands for 100 miles. How many miles do two inches stand for?

Step 3 It is about five inches on the map from Pittsburgh to Plymouth. So the distance from the real city of Pittsburgh to Plymouth must be about 500 miles.

Practice the Skill

Look at the map. Follow the directions to find distances. Use a ruler.

 About how many inches is it on the map from Plymouth to Washington, D.C.?

 How many miles is it from Plymouth to Washington, D.C.? Use the scale to find out.

 A truck carries clams from Plymouth to Ithaca. How many miles does the truck travel?

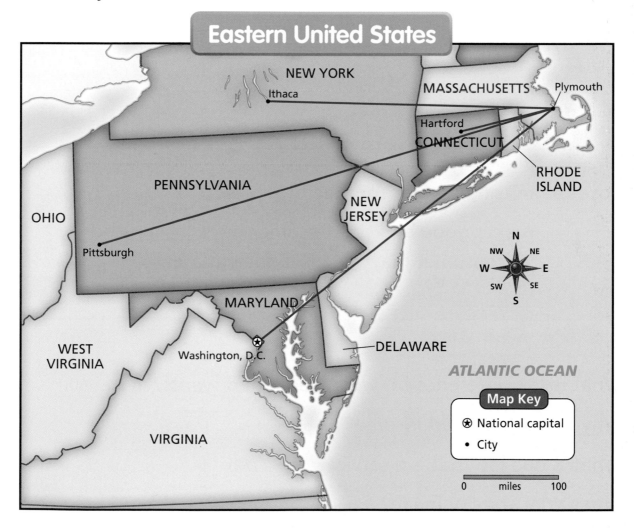

Eastern United States

NEW YORK

Ithaca

MASSACHUSETTS

Plymouth

Hartford

CONNECTICUT

RHODE ISLAND

PENNSYLVANIA

NEW JERSEY

OHIO

Pittsburgh

N

NW   NE

W   E

SW   SE

S

MARYLAND

WEST VIRGINIA

Washington, D.C.

DELAWARE

ATLANTIC OCEAN

Map Key

⊛ National capital

• City

VIRGINIA

0   miles   100

Big Ideas

The Big Idea

Producers and Consumers

makes → goods

Producer

buys

buys → services

Consumer saves

Choose the missing words from the organizer.

1. A _____ makes goods.   2. A consumer buys _____ and services.   3. A consumer may _____ money in a bank.

Facts and Main Ideas

4. What is the difference between needs and wants? (page 160)

5. Why do people need income? (page 168)

6. What is one job that is a service? (page 173)

7. What does **scarcity** mean? (page 192)

Vocabulary

Use words from the box to complete the sentences.

Consumers earn **8.** _____
to pay for needs and **9.** _____ .
One need is **10.** _____ .
Consumers look at the
11. _____ of goods and
12. _____ . Consumers may
save money in a **13.** _____
to pay later for things they want.

A. prices (page 180)

B. income (page 168)

C. savings account
(page 182)

D. services (page 173)

E. specialize (page 199)

F. wants (page 160)

G. shelter (page 160)

✔ Test Practice

14. What does the word **barter** mean?

A. earning a small income

B. saving money in a bank

C. trading without money

D. producing many goods

Critical Thinking

Main Idea and Details

15. What are two examples of human resources?

16. What are two examples of trade?

Skillbuilders **Use a Map Scale**

Route to Airport

17. On this map, one inch equals _____ .

18. How far is it from Maria's house to the airport?

Read a Bar Graph

19. Which place at school has the fewest workers?

20. How many workers are in the office and the cafeteria all together?

Number of Workers in Our School

Unit Activity

Make a Mobile

If you earned $10, how much of your money would you spend and save?

① Write and draw your choices.

② Make sure that they add up to $10.

③ Cut out your choices and hang them up to make a mobile. Explain your choices.

Save $2.00 in bank

Spend $4.00 on cat toy

Spend $4.00 on colored pencils

Current Events Project

Publish a class newspaper about people at work around the world. Use information from the Weekly Reader at the Social Studies Website.

JOBS AROUND THE WORLD

Rug weaving   Fishing

Technology

Current Events Project
For current events information go to
www.eduplace.com/kids/hmss05/

In Your Classroom

Look for these Social Studies Independent Books in your classroom.

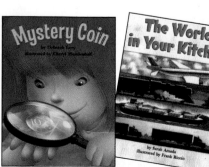

At the Library

You may find these books at your school or public library.

Follow the Money
by Loreen Leedy

The Paperboy
by Dav Pilkey

UNIT 5

America's Past

The Big Idea

Why is the past important to you today?

Unit 5 · America's Past

Vocabulary Preview

Technology

e • glossary
e • word games
www.eduplace.com/kids/hmss05/

explorer

We remember Christopher Columbus, an **explorer** who traveled to find new things and places. page 222

colonist

A **colonist** is a person who lives in a colony. Many colonists came to America seeking freedom. page 230

Reading Strategy

Use the **predict and infer** reading strategy in Lessons 1, 2, 3, and 4 and the **monitor and clarify** strategy in Lessons 5, 6, and 7.

independence

The 13 colonies gained independence from Great Britain. **Independence** is freedom from the rule of another nation. page 242

technology

Technology is the use of science to make new things or to make things work better. page 260

Vocabulary
history

Reading Skill
Classify

First Americans

Build on What You Know How old are you? Your age now is in the present. You will be a grownup in the future. You were a baby in the past.

History

You remember things that happened in the past. Also you learn about the past from family stories. **History** is everything we can know about the past. History is everything that happened in the lives of people from far back in the past up to the present.

main (★) *idea*

A storyteller in Alaska uses his drum to tell a traditional tale to young people.

The First People in America

Our country's history starts with American main idea Indians. Hundreds of American Indian groups already lived in America more than 500 years ago. They depended on natural resources. American Indians used water, land, and plants in many different ways. Their clothes, tools, and other things from the past help us learn about their lives.

This map locates just four of the many groups of American Indians. They are the four you will learn about on the next pages.

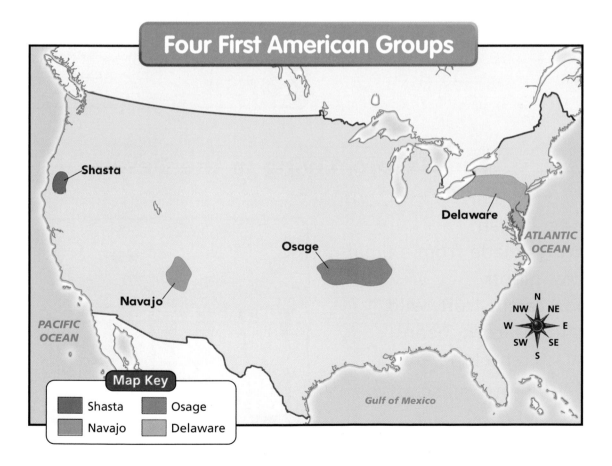

Four First American Groups

Shasta

Delaware

ATLANTIC OCEAN

Osage

Navajo

PACIFIC OCEAN

N
NW   NE
W   E
SW   SE
S

Gulf of Mexico

Map Key

Shasta   Osage
Navajo   Delaware

Skill **Reading Maps** Which group was in the northwest?

Compare Groups

The Delaware, Living in Woodlands

Homes winter longhouse for several families; summer wigwam for each family
Clothes made from deerskin
Food nuts, berries, corn, beans, squash, deer meat
Travel by canoe, on foot

The Navajo, Living in the Desert

Home hogan
Clothes made from animal skins, plants
Food cactus fruit, wild potatoes, corn, beans, squash, antelope and deer meat
Travel on foot

The Osage, Living on the Plains

Homes winter longhouses for several families, small summer homes for travelers
Clothes made from deerskin
Food nuts, plums, grapes, potatoes, corn, beans, pumpkins, turkey, buffalo
Travel on foot, by canoe

The Shasta, Living Near the Ocean

Homes winter dwelling house for several families, summer cool brush shelter
Clothes made from animal skins, fur, braided grass
Food bulbs, berries, pine nuts, acorns, turtles, grasshoppers, fish, deer, elk
Travel on foot, with snowshoes in winter, by canoe

Natural Resources and Daily Life

These pictures show some things that American Indians made and used hundreds of years ago. People in the present might see these things in a museum. American Indians used many natural resources to make the things they needed.

(⭐) main idea

Navajo sandals were made from braided leaves of desert plants.

The Osage and other groups who lived on the plains wove baskets from long grasses.

Some American Indian groups in plains and woodlands made dugout canoes from logs of trees.

Review Where might people today see things that people made hundreds of years ago?

Lesson Review

❶ **Vocabulary** Write a sentence that uses the words **history** and **American Indian.**

❷ **Main Idea** Why were natural resources important to American Indians?

✏️ **Activity** Choose two groups and tell a way they were alike and a way they were different.

The Young Woman and the Thunder Beings

This legend is retold by Joseph Bruchac in his book Between Earth and Sky. **In the past, the Seneca told this story. In the present they still tell it. Read it to see why.**

To the North lived the Longhouse People, near the edge of the falls called Ne-ah-ga.

They sometimes spoke of the Thunder Beings who lived in a cave beneath the falls. When a child wanted to give thanks to the Thunderers for the gift of rain, he would place an offering in a canoe and put it in the river to float over the falls.

One day a young woman alone in her canoe, was crossing the river far up from the falls when she lost her paddle. The current was swift and she found herself swept away. This brave young woman had always been a friend of the Thunderers, giving them gifts with each new season. So, as she fell, she did not scream or cry. In trust, she asked calmly for help.

The Thunder Beings saved her life, catching her safely in their blanket. Then the chief of the Thunderers asked the young woman to be his wife. She agreed, and to this day, the Seneca say that when the rumbling voices of the Thunder Beings roll across the sky, the brave young woman is keeping watch, reminding us that every gift we give gives us back a blessing.

Activities

1. **Talk About It** Is this a true story? Explain why or why not.

2. **Act It Out** List the characters in the story and act out what they do.

▶ **Vocabulary**
explorer
journey

◎ **Reading Skill**
Compare and Contrast

Explorers Travel the World

Build on What You Know Have you traveled to a place that was new to you? What did you learn about it?

Explorers from Europe

An **explorer** is a person who travels to find out new things. A **journey** is a trip. Many hundreds of years ago, explorers from Europe made journeys to other lands. They did not have cars, planes, or steam engines then. Their maps did not show much about the places they were going. Their journeys were filled with adventures.

main idea (★)

Marco Polo

Marco Polo

More than 700 years ago, a man from Italy named Marco Polo traveled to Asia. He spent many years in China. He told thrilling stories about new things he saw on his journeys. His stories were put into a book. Most people in Europe knew nothing about what Asia was like. Marco Polo's stories made them want to find out more.

Marco Polo in the court of the Chinese emperor

Review Why was Marco Polo important in history?

Route from Europe to Asia

EUROPE
Venice

ASIA
Shangdu
Beijing
Kashgar

Mediterranean Sea

CHINA

AFRICA

INDIA

Map Key
→ Marco Polo's route
⌃⌃ Mountains

0   2,000 kilometers
0   2,000 miles

N
NW   NE
W   E
SW   SE
S

INDIAN
OCEAN

Christopher Columbus

Christopher Columbus was an explorer from Europe who wanted to find a faster way to reach parts of Asia. Columbus read Marco Polo's stories and studied many maps. He decided to sail west across the Atlantic Ocean. His ships reached land that he thought was Asia. Explorers who came later learned that it was not Asia. It was another continent—now called North America.

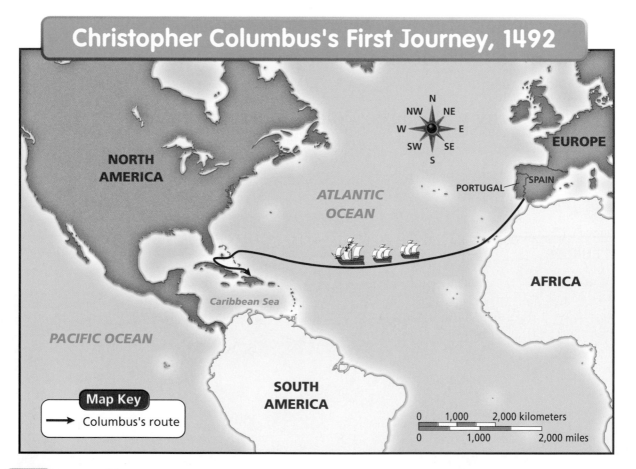

Christopher Columbus's First Journey, 1492

NORTH AMERICA

EUROPE

ATLANTIC OCEAN

PORTUGAL

SPAIN

AFRICA

Caribbean Sea

PACIFIC OCEAN

SOUTH AMERICA

Map Key
→ Columbus's route

0   1,000   2,000 kilometers
0   1,000   2,000 miles

Skill **Reading Maps** What ocean did Christopher Columbus cross?

Christopher Columbus set out from Spain with a crew of ninety sailors in three ships, the **Niña**, **Pinta**, and **Santa Maria**.

The journeys of Christopher Columbus changed what people knew about the world. North America and South America soon became part of the world map for Europeans. The new knowledge led to other changes for people who lived in the Americas.

Christopher Columbus

Review Why did Christopher Columbus sail west?

Lesson Review

❶ **Vocabulary** Write a sentence that uses the words **journey** and **explorer.**

❷ **Main Idea** Why was Marco Polo's journey important to Christopher Columbus?

Activity Write or tell a way that Marco Polo and Christopher Columbus were alike and a way they were different.

The Magnetic Compass

How did Christopher Columbus find his way across the Atlantic Ocean? A magnetic compass helped him.

A magnetic compass is like a compass rose. It shows directions: north, south, east and west. But a magnetic compass has something more. It has a needle that is a magnet. Because the needle is a magnet, it always points towards the earth's North Pole. Once you know where north is, you can find east, south, and west too.

People in China were the first to make magnetic compasses.

Read a Magnetic Compass

1 Rest the compass on a table.
Find the colored end of the needle.
That end points north.

2 Locate the letters N, E, S, and W.
Name the direction word that each letter
stands for.

3 Gently turn the compass until the needle is in line
with the letter N. What does the needle do when
you turn the compass?

4 Hold both arms out together ahead of you and face
the direction that the compass points. You should
be facing and pointing north.

Jamestown and Plymouth

Vocabulary

colony
settlement
colonist
Pilgrim

Reading Skill

Compare and Contrast

Build on What You Know How would you feel about moving to a place far away?

American Land

After Columbus, more explorers from Europe traveled to other parts of North America. They hoped to find gold and other riches. They saw great natural resources in the forests, plains, and rivers. American Indians already lived there. But kings and queens from countries in Europe wanted the land for their countries. They sent people to settle in North America.

English Colonies

A **colony** is a place that is ruled by another country. England was one of the countries that started colonies in North America. People from England traveled in ships to settle there. Their colonies began with small communities called **settlements.** The map shows two of the earliest settlements. See what you can learn about Plymouth and Jamestown from the map.

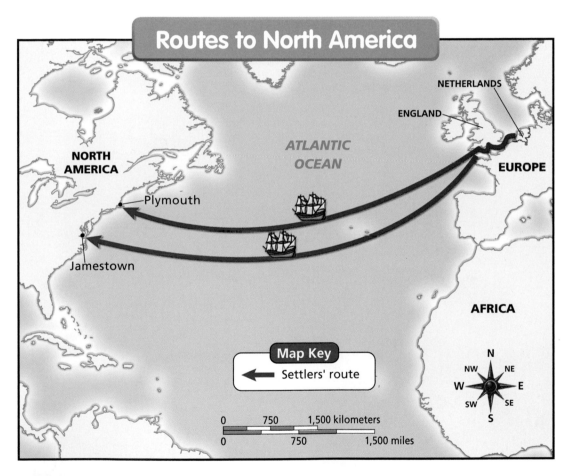

Routes to North America

NETHERLANDS

ENGLAND

ATLANTIC OCEAN

NORTH AMERICA

EUROPE

Plymouth

Jamestown

AFRICA

Map Key

← Settlers' route

N
NW · NE
W — E
SW · SE
S

0   750   1,500 kilometers

0   750   1,500 miles

Skill **Reading Maps** Why do you think both settlements were built near water?

Jamestown

A **colonist** is a person who lives in a colony. The first colonists in Jamestown were men and boys. They worked hard to stay alive. The colonists cut down trees, which they used to build a fort and some houses.

At first they did not have enough food. They ate fish and turtles, even raccoons. Nearby American Indians called the Pamunkey gave them some corn. Also, the colonists had copper that they traded for corn. The Pamunkey wanted the copper to make jewelry.

Later the colonists sent for others in their families. Life was hard for everyone. Children worked along with grownups.

Soon the colonists at Jamestown began to produce goods, such as lumber and window glass. They sent these products to be sold in England.

Skill **Visual Learning** What are some things in the picture that show what colonists in Jamestown did?

Plymouth

Many of the first colonists at Plymouth belonged to the same religious group. They became known as **Pilgrims.** The Pilgrims came to America because they wanted freedom to follow their religious beliefs. Whole families came together. In the first year, they faced sickness, fire, and freezing weather. American Indians called the Wampanoag (wahm puh NOH ag) helped the Pilgrims. The Wampanoag showed the Pilgrims how to plant, hunt, and fish.

Everyone had to help out. Girls and boys helped cook, clean, and look after the younger children. Women kept the gardens. They made and mended the family's clothes. They taught the children to read and write. Men built homes. They hunted and fished and planted corn.

Review In what ways was daily life in Plymouth like daily life in Jamestown?

Lesson Review

❶ Vocabulary Use the words **Pilgrim** and **colony** to tell something you have learned.

❷ Main Idea What did colonists from England need to do to live in their new settlements?

Activity Write a description of a way that American Indians helped colonists from England.

Readers' Theater

The Mayflower Crossing

What was the ocean crossing like for the Pilgrims aboard the **Mayflower**? Follow them on their journey from England to America.

Characters

Narrator

Mary Brewster: woman

Love Brewster: Mary's son

Constance Hopkins: girl

William Bradford: man

Rose Standish: woman

Elizabeth Tilley: girl

Thomas English: sailor

Scene 1

Narrator: It is September 10, 1620. The **Mayflower** has been at sea for four days.

Love: I am so tired of looking at the ocean, Mother.

Mary: Be patient. There are many days ahead on this little ship.

Thomas: Better go below! A storm is coming! You will find it a little too exciting on deck!

Scene 2

Narrator: Two weeks pass. The sea grows rougher.

Constance: I wish this awful rolling would stop!

Rose: If we only had fresh water.

Love: Or a hot meal. Even beans would do.

Mary: Be glad we have cheese and biscuits.

Elizabeth: Father says the main beam of the ship has cracked.

William: Don't worry. The sailors are fixing it.

Thomas: We'll use these tools to pull the beam together.

Scene 3

Narrator: Halfway through the crossing, during a storm, a cry goes up.

Thomas: Help! John Howland has washed overboard!

Elizabeth: He fell from the main deck!

Love: Wait! He has grabbed hold of a rope.

Elizabeth: They are lifting him out! He is safe, thank goodness.

William: Listen. There is another cry: a new-born baby!

Constance: Mother has had a baby boy. She has named him Oceanus. They are both doing well.

All: Congratulations!

William: This news should give us all hope.

Scene 4

Narrator: In November, more than nine weeks after leaving England, we hear the call we've been waiting for.

Thomas: Land!

Elizabeth: I see it! A long curving beach.

Rose: My husband, Miles, will bring men ashore.

William: We will look for a good place to build our community.

Love: Fresh water!

Rose and Mary: Clean clothes!

William: Friends, it is time to begin our new lives.

Activities

1. **Think About It** What do you think was most difficult for the passengers of the **Mayflower?**

2. **Write About It** Write a letter you might have sent to England if you had sailed on the **Mayflower.**

Identify Cause and Effect

▶ **Vocabulary**

cause
effect

The Pilgrims wanted to land at the Hudson River. They thought the river was part of Virginia. Why did they land on Cape Cod? Knowing about cause and effect can help you understand what happened.

Learn the Skill

A **cause** makes something happen. Something that happens is an **effect**.

Step 1 Look at this map. The star shows the place the Pilgrims wanted to land. The dot shows where the Pilgrims really landed.

Step 2 Use the map to find one thing that caused the **Mayflower** to change its route. The map shows that one cause was a storm.

Step 3 You can explain cause and effect using the word **because**. The **Mayflower** changed its route because it hit a storm.

Practice the Skill

Follow the directions to identify cause and effect.

1 After the **Mayflower** left Cape Cod for the Hudson River, what caused the ship to turn around and go back?

2 Think about what you have learned. What are two causes for why the Pilgrims landed on Cape Cod?

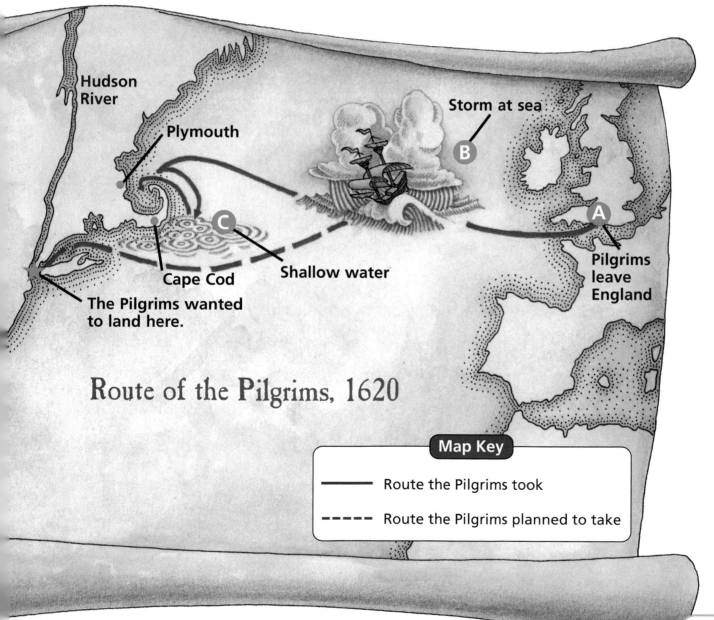

Hudson River

Plymouth

Storm at sea

B

Cape Cod

Shallow water

The Pilgrims wanted to land here.

A

Pilgrims leave England

C

Route of the Pilgrims, 1620

Map Key

———— Route the Pilgrims took

- - - - - Route the Pilgrims planned to take

A New Country

Build on What You Know Have you had to follow rules that didn't seem fair to you?

Many Colonies

After the first settlements in Jamestown and Plymouth, more people came from England to settle in North America. They built homes and churches. They started farms and businesses. Some small communities grew into large towns and cities. People worked and planned together. But they had to follow rules from the king of England, who was the ruler of Great Britain and its colonies.

The map shows thirteen of the colonies in North America in 1763.

Review What were the names of the colonies?

The Thirteen Colonies

NEW HAMPSHIRE
MASSACHUSETTS
NEW YORK
RHODE ISLAND
CONNECTICUT
PENNSYLVANIA
NEW JERSEY
DELAWARE
MARYLAND
VIRGINIA
NORTH CAROLINA
SOUTH CAROLINA
GEORGIA

ATLANTIC OCEAN

Boston

Charleston

Philadelphia

Independence

Independence means being free from rule by another nation. <u>More and more colonists in America wanted independence from Great Britain.</u> Some colonists began to act against British rules and taxes. One group of colonists acted against a tax on tea. Their action was called the Boston Tea Party. King George ruled Great Britain then. He sent more and more armies to control the colonists.

Look at events on the timeline.

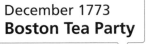

December 1773
Boston Tea Party

April 1775
British army fights with colonists in Massachusetts

1770   1773   1775

The Declaration of Independence

People from the thirteen colonies did not all agree about independence from Great Britain. Each colony sent people to Philadelphia to meet and make a decision. People at the meeting chose Thomas Jefferson to write words explaining why the colonies wanted independence. Those words became the Declaration of Independence. By signing the Declaration of Independence, colonists came together for the goal of independence.

(★ main idea)

Review What did colonists do that showed they wanted independence?

July 1776
Thirteen colonies agree on the Declaration of Independence

1776

1780

This painting shows an artist's idea of how George Washington looked when he crossed the Delaware River during the American Revolution.

The American Revolution

Great Britain would not allow independence. King George sent soldiers to fight a war against the colonists. The war was called the American Revolution. George Washington led the soldiers who fought against Britain. There were terrible battles. The American Revolution lasted eight years. Finally in 1783, the war ended. The colonies had won independence. They became a country called the United States of America.

Leaders for Independence

You have read how George Washington and Thomas Jefferson helped America gain independence. Many others helped too. **Benjamin Franklin** got colonists to think and talk about why they wanted independence. **Abigail Adams** wrote what she saw and thought about the fight for independence. **Samuel Adams** made speeches that got many colonists to fight for independence. **Paul Revere** helped colonists work together against Great Britain.

Benjamin Franklin

Review Why did colonists fight in the American Revolution?

Samuel Adams

Lesson Review

HANDS ON

❶ **Vocabulary** Use the word **independence** in a sentence about colonists.

❷ **Main Idea** Why was the Declaration of Independence important to the colonists?

Activity Draw a picture of a person or an event that helped America become an independent country. Tell why that person or event was important.

Two Patriots

Abigail Adams and Paul Revere both used their minds and hands to help win independence for their country.

Abigail Adams

Abigail Adams always loved to write long letters. She described events in exciting detail and shared her own ideas.

Abigail married John Adams, who was a leader in the American Revolution. He often traveled far from home. Abigail wrote to him daily. She described life with their children and troubles from the war. Abigail also explained her own ideas about independence.

1776
Wrote about importance of women

1744
Born in Weymouth, Massachusetts

1818
Died

1700

1800

In this letter, Abigail Adams told John to "remember the ladies..." in the fight for independence.

Paul Revere

Paul Revere boldly joined other colonists who showed they were against British rule. He kept on doing many things to fight for independence.

At night on April 18, 1775, Paul Revere rode his horse from Boston to warn colonists of a British army plan. This prepared colonists in Lexington to fight a battle that became known as the start of the American Revolution. His brave ride became famous in a poem by Henry Wadsworth Longfellow.

1735
Born in Boston, Massachusetts

1775
Rode to warn about British

1818
Died

1700

1800

A picture book of Longfellow's poem

Activities

1. **Write About It** Write or tell two ways that Paul Revere and Abigail Adams showed **patriotism.**

2. **Make It** Make a poster that shows something important about the life of Abigail Adams or Paul Revere.

Skillbuilder

Compare Fact and Opinion

▶ **Vocabulary**

fact

opinion

A **fact** is something that is true. An **opinion** is what someone thinks. Two people can have different opinions about the same facts.

Learn the Skill

Step 1 Read the sentences about Independence Day. One sentence tells a fact. The other sentence tells an opinion.

> Independence Day is on July 4 every year.

> I think Independence Day is the best national holiday.

Step 2 A fact is something that is true. You can check to see if a fact is true. A fact is probably true if two or more good nonfiction books agree.

Step 3 Opinions use words such as "I think."

Practice the Skill

Read the sentences. Then follow the directions.

1 In what way is a fact different from an opinion?

2 Which sentences below tell facts?

3 Which sentence below tells an opinion? Tell how you know that it is an opinion.

George Washington was the first President of our country.

John Hancock's signature is the largest on the Declaration of Independence.

I think Benjamin Franklin was the greatest inventor of all time.

Past Heroes

Build on What You Know Think of a person who is special.

Heroes

A **hero** is someone who does something brave for the good of others or works hard to help others. Some heroes are strong leaders of a group. Some heroes are inventors. An inventor is someone who finds new ways to do things. Look at some heroes from the past. They were important to people in the past, and they are still important today.

Vocabulary
hero
invention

Reading Skill
Classify

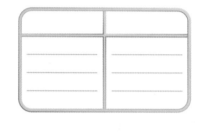

main idea ★

★ Sitting Bull ★

Sitting Bull was a leader of the Lakota nation. He was known for being powerful, brave, and wise. He believed strongly in Lakota traditions.

(★) main idea

Sitting Bull was against the United States control of Lakota land. He helped the Lakota nation to fight the United States Army. He always stood firmly for a way of life he felt was right.

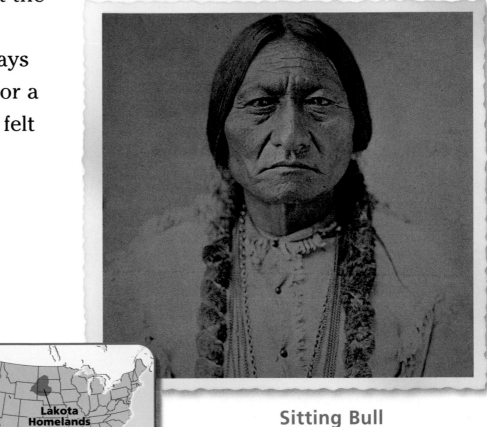

Lakota Homelands

Sitting Bull

Review Why is Sitting Bull still a hero?

★ Golda Meir ★

Golda Meir was a Jewish immigrant from
Russia to the United States. As a young woman,
she joined others who worked to start a Jewish
nation called Israel. Golda Meir gave strong speeches.
She worked hard to start the new nation. <u>Golda
Meir was a leader of Israel.</u> She was one of the first
women to lead a country.

main idea (★)

Golda Meir

★ Jackie Robinson ★

Jackie Robinson was excellent in many sports. In 1947, he became the first African American baseball player in the National League. At that time, many people did not want African American players to be with white players. They did hurtful things to make him quit. But Jackie Robinson did not quit. He kept playing baseball. He set a great example. Other African American players began to join teams with white players.

Jackie Robinson

Review What are some ways that Jackie Robinson, Golda Meir, and Sitting Bull are alike?

★ Thomas Edison ★

Thomas Edison was a great inventor. Even as a boy, he loved to try out new ideas. He learned science on his own. In his life, he produced more than a thousand inventions. An **invention** is something new that someone makes or thinks of. Two of Thomas Edison's inventions were the electric light bulb and sound recordings. These inventions changed people's daily lives.

Thomas Edison

★ Albert Einstein ★

Albert Einstein grew up in Germany. As a young child, he was excited by science questions. As an adult, Albert Einstein kept thinking about science. He explained how light works. He changed ideas in science about time and space. <u>His work helped people understand the world.</u>

main idea (★)

Review What is a way that Albert Einstein and Thomas Edison are alike?

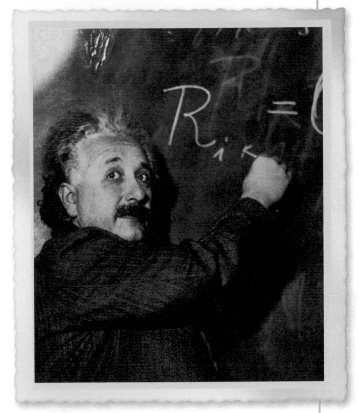

Albert Einstein

Lesson Review

❶ **Vocabulary** Write a sentence that tells why one of the people you have read about is a **hero.**

❷ **Main Idea** Why are heroes from the past still important to people today?

▶ **Activity** Choose a hero in the lesson. Write or tell two things the hero could feel proud about.

LEARN FROM A LETTER

Do you like to save letters or cards from people you know? Branch Rickey saved a thank-you letter from Jackie Robinson. Now, more than fifty years later, we can learn from it.

Branch Rickey was the manager of the Brooklyn Dodgers baseball team. When he hired Jackie Robinson for the Dodgers, some people said that the team was headed for big trouble. Jackie Robinson wrote this letter after three years of great playing for the Dodgers. He wrote because Branch Rickey was leaving the team.

HOTEL *Jaragua*

CIUDAD TRUJILLO • REPUBLICA DOMINICANA

. . . It has been the finest experience I have had being associated [a friend] with you and I want to thank you very much for all you have meant not only to me and my family but to the entire country and particularly [mostly to] members of our race. . . .

My wife joins me in saying thanks very much Mr. Rickey. . .

Sincerely yours,

Jackie Robinson

Activities

1. **Talk About It** What did Branch Rickey do to show respect for Jackie Robinson?

2. **Write About It** Name someone you would like to thank. Write a letter to the person with your reasons for thanking him or her.

Communities Change

Vocabulary

transportation
technology

Reading Skill

Sequence

Build on What You Know What are some ways that you have traveled? Do you think those ways were possible for people two hundred years ago?

Transportation

Transportation is any way of moving things or people from one place to another. When people travel or move goods, they use transportation.

Technology is using science to make things work better. Inventors have used technology to make transportation faster, stronger, and safer. Technology has helped them make new kinds of transportation. New kinds of transportation have changed how people live in a community.

main idea

The two maps show changes in one community: Plainfield, Illinois. Compare the roads on both maps.

Illinois

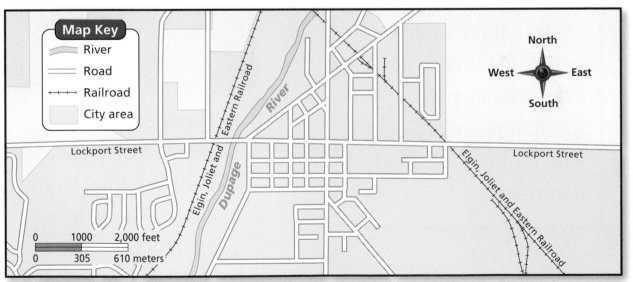

Plainfield, Illinois, more than 100 years ago

Plainfield today

Review What is a way that technology has changed communities?

Transportation Changes Plainfield

Look at some changes in transportation that brought more people and business to this community.

1850   1900

1834

People came by stagecoach to settle in the new town. Stagecoaches also brought travelers who stopped for food and rest.

1904

People rode streetcars on railways between towns. Many came to Plainfield for vacations in a place called Electric Park.

1920

The first paved highway to cross the country went through Plainfield. Cars and buses brought more people. Trucks brought goods quickly. More businesses opened.

Review What were three kinds of transportation that went through Plainfield?

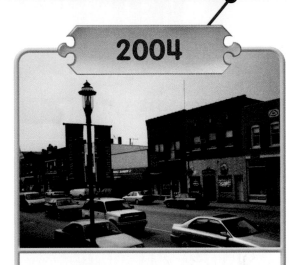

2004

Now many highways go around and through Plainfield. It is a suburb of Chicago. People have built more homes and schools. Families keep moving to Plainfield.

Lesson Review

❶ **Vocabulary** Tell a way that technology has changed transportation.

❷ **Main Idea** Give an example of how transportation changed Plainfield.

➤ **Activity** Name a kind of transportation that people use today. Explain how it helps people.

Two Inventors

Both inventors found new ways to do things in transportation.

Granville T. Woods

Train crashes were a big problem when Granville T. Woods was a young man. He invented a Railway Telegraph that located moving trains. It kept trains from crashing. Granville T. Woods invented much more. He invented a grooved wheel that allowed a street car, or trolley, to receive electricity to move it along tracks. Granville T. Woods started a company to make and sell his inventions.

Taylor G. Wang

Taylor Wang is a scientist, an inventor, and a college teacher. He wanted to find new ways for scientists to work in space. To do this he became an astronaut. He set up a science lab on the space shuttle. During the flight he was always solving problems in the lab. Taylor Wang and other scientists still use what he learned in space.

Activities

1. **Act It Out** Act out or describe something Granville T. Woods or Taylor Wang did as an inventor.

2. **List It** Make a list of facts about Granville T. Woods and another list of facts about Taylor G. Wang. Use the lists to compare the two inventors.

Understand Point of View

▶ **Vocabulary**

point of view

A **point of view** is what someone thinks about something. When people give reasons for what they think, they help others understand their point of view.

Learn the Skill

Step 1 Read this question. **What do you think was the best invention in transportation? Tell why.**

Step 2 Read two different points of view.

- **Jeff:** I think the railroad train was best, because more people could travel across land after that.
- **Sheera:** I think the airplane was the best invention. Flying helped people get places much faster.

Step 3 Both Jeff and Sheera gave reasons for their points of view. Tell two ways their points of view are different.

Practice the Skill

1 Look at the pictures of inventions in transportation below. Which do you think was the best invention?

2 Give your answer. Make sure to tell a reason for your point of view.

3 Tell a way that your point of view is different from Jeff's or Sheera's or the point of view of someone in your class.

Communication Changes

Build on What You Know What are some ways that you can leave a message for someone? Which of those ways were possible 200 years ago?

Communication in History

Communication is any way of sharing information. Communication has changed over the years. *(main idea)*

Mail by Stagecoach

In 1776, Benjamin Franklin headed the American postal system. He got stagecoaches to carry mail between post offices. This helped letters reach people faster.

Telegraph

In 1844, an American, Samuel Morse, invented a telegraph system. People could then send messages along a wire. They used a code of clicks to stand for letters of the alphabet. They could send news quickly along hundreds of miles of wire.

Telephone

In 1876, Alexander Graham Bell showed how people could send voice messages along a wire. These were the first telephones. Once telephone wires were strung across the country, people could talk even if they lived far apart.

Review In what way were the telegraph system and postal system alike?

Radio

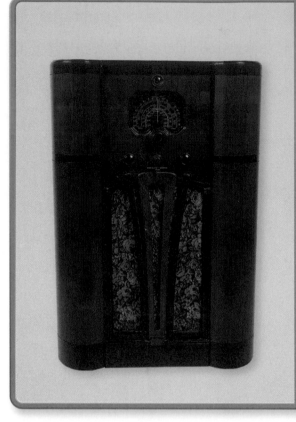

By 1900, inventors had used technology to send messages by airwaves. This led to the radio. Over time, people began to have radios at home. Families around the country could listen to the same music, news, or speeches. People heard plays, comedies, and stories too.

Television

In 1938, inventors showed how people could hear and see events live on television. Then some inventors found ways to make it work well in homes. By the 1950's many families had television.

Internet

By 1975, inventors had ways to connect computers. They called these networks. People could send messages between computers in a network. Soon computers around the world could join one huge network called the Internet. What can you do on the Internet?

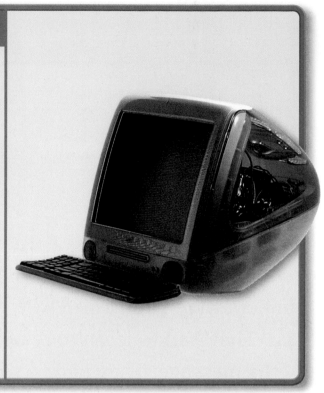

Review In what ways were radio and television alike?

Lesson Review

1. **Vocabulary** Use the word **communication** in a sentence about something you use now.

2. **Main Idea** Give two examples of something that changed communication after 1775.

  Activity Choose one of the ways of communicating shown in this lesson. Make a chart comparing it with something you use now.

Communication: Runners with a Message

Long ago in South America people called the Incas got messages from runners. The runners were young men who trained to run very fast. They had to learn to remember every word of the message. They had to speak it very clearly. One runner started with a message. He ran for miles along a road to a spot where another runner waited. Each runner had to listen closely and then run on with the message. What could happen if one runner did not listen well?

Inca pots had paintings of Inca runners.

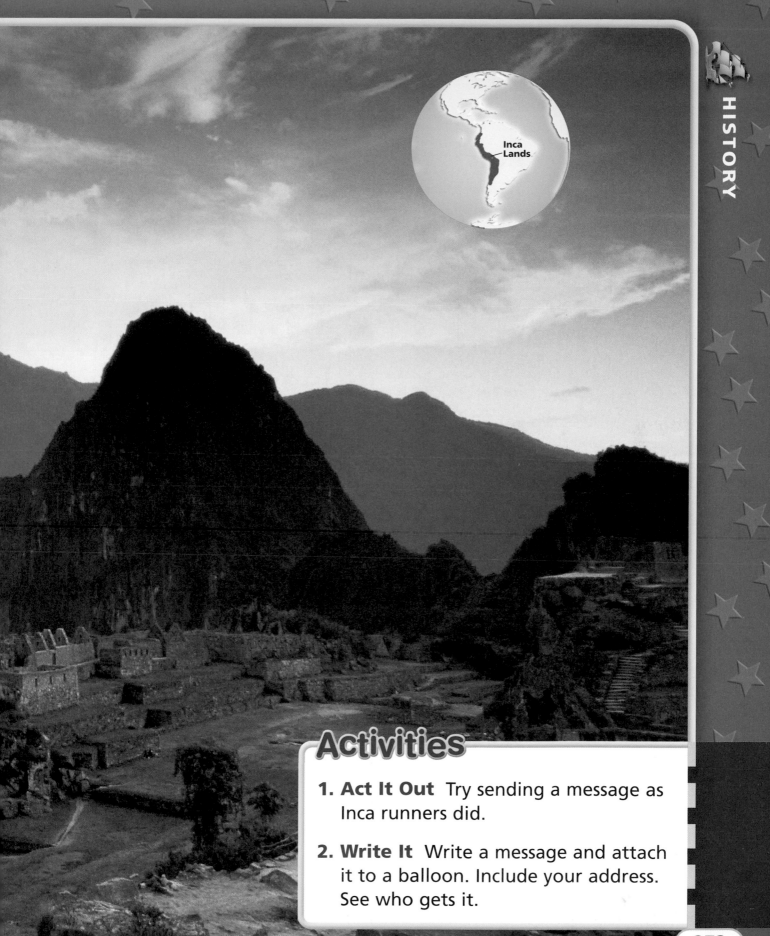

Inca
Lands

Activities

1. **Act It Out** Try sending a message as Inca runners did.

2. **Write It** Write a message and attach it to a balloon. Include your address. See who gets it.

Timeline in American History

1492 1607 1776

1400 1500 1600 1700 1800

American Indian communities

Explorers come from Europe

Settlers come from Europe

American colonists want independence

Find the missing words on the timeline.

1. _____ lived in America before explorers came.

2. _____ came after explorers from Europe.

3. In 1776, _____ said they wanted independence.

Facts and Main Ideas

4. What was a food that American Indians ate? (pages 214, 215)

5. Name two kinds of work the Plymouth colonists did. (pages 232, 233)

6. Name two leaders who wanted independence from Great Britain. (pages 243, 244, 245)

7. Who were two American inventors? (pages 256, 257, 264, 265)

Vocabulary

Choose the letter of the word that best matches the picture.

8.

9.

10.

11.

12.

A. **explorer** (page 222)

B. **colonist** (page 230)

C. **settlement** (page 230)

D. **communication**
(page 268)

E. **transportation**
(page 260)

✔ **Test Practice**

13. What does the word **history** mean?

A. a long trip
B. a Plymouth colonist
C. everything you can know about the past
D. new things people make or think of

Critical Thinking

Sequence

14. Who came first? Who came next? List these people in
time order.
a. Christopher Columbus   **b.** Marco Polo   **c.** Thomas Jefferson

Skillbuilders   Identify Cause and Effect

Read the paragraph and answer the questions.

When colonists in America wanted independence, the king of England sent the British army to control them. More colonists became angry at the actions of the king. They decided to fight for independence.

The Beginning of the American Revolution

15. Why did the king of England send armies to America?

16. Why did the colonists fight the British army?

Compare Fact and Opinion

A fact is something that is true. An opinion is what someone thinks.

17. Which sentence tells a fact?

18. Which sentence is an opinion? Tell if you agree or disagree.

A. I think it would be fun to sail on the **Mayflower.**

B. The **Mayflower** landed in America in 1620.

Unit Activity

The Big Idea

Make a History Puppet

Choose a person from American history and make a puppet of that person.

❶ Make the puppet's head and costume.

❷ Write three questions that you would like people to ask your puppet.

❸ Use your hand and voice so that your puppet answers the questions.

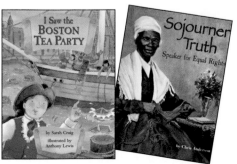

In Your Classroom

Look for these Social Studies Independent Books in your classroom.

WEEKLY (WR) READER

Current Events Project

Make a timeline of events in the news. Use information from the Weekly Reader at the Social Studies Website.

MONUMENT TIMELINE

2002 2003 2004 2005 2006

February 2002 Monument plans

June 2004 Building begins

October 2006 Monument done

Technology

Current Events Project
For current events information, go to
www.eduplace.com/kids/hmss05/

At the Library

You may find these books at your school or public library.

Life in a Colonial Town
by Sally Senzell Isaacs

Thomas Edison
by Lola Schaefer

277

America's Government

"My country 'tis of thee,
Sweet land of liberty,
Of thee I sing."

—Samuel Francis Smith
from "America"

The Big Idea

What does government mean to you and your family?

Vocabulary Preview

 Technology
e • **glossary**
e • **word games**
www.eduplace.com/kids/hmss05/

government

Government is a group of people who make and carry out laws. **page 283**

citizen

A **citizen** is a member of a community, state, or country. You are a citizen of your class too. **page 292**

Reading Strategy

Use the **summarize** reading strategy in Lessons 1, 2, and 3 and the **question** strategy in Lessons 4, 5, and 6.

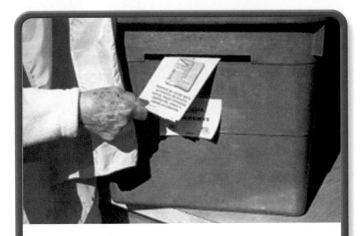

election

An **election** is a time when people vote. You can hold a class election to make a choice. page 308

Constitution

The **Constitution** is a plan for making rules for the United States government. page 316

Government and People

Vocabulary

government
capital
tax

 Reading Skill

Draw Conclusions

Build on What You Know

Who are the people who help run your school? What are some ways they work together?

Communities are like schools. A community needs a group of people working together to help it run well.

A school principal raises the flag with the help of students.

Most communities have a city or town hall building where people work to run local government.

Local Government

A **government** is a group of people who work together to run a community, state, or country. The government of a community is called a local government. People in your local government decide how to use money for schools, police, and other community needs. They try to solve community problems too.

main idea (★)

Review What do people in government do?

Three Governments

Your state also has a government. Each state has a **capital,** which is a city where the people in government work. The United States has a government, too. That is the national government. It is in Washington, D.C., the nation's capital. Everyone has three governments: local, state, and national.

Look at Robin, for example.

I live in Duluth, Minnesota. Leaders of my **local** government meet in Duluth.

Leaders of my **state** government meet in St. Paul, the capital of Minnesota.

Leaders of my **national** government meet in Washington, D.C.

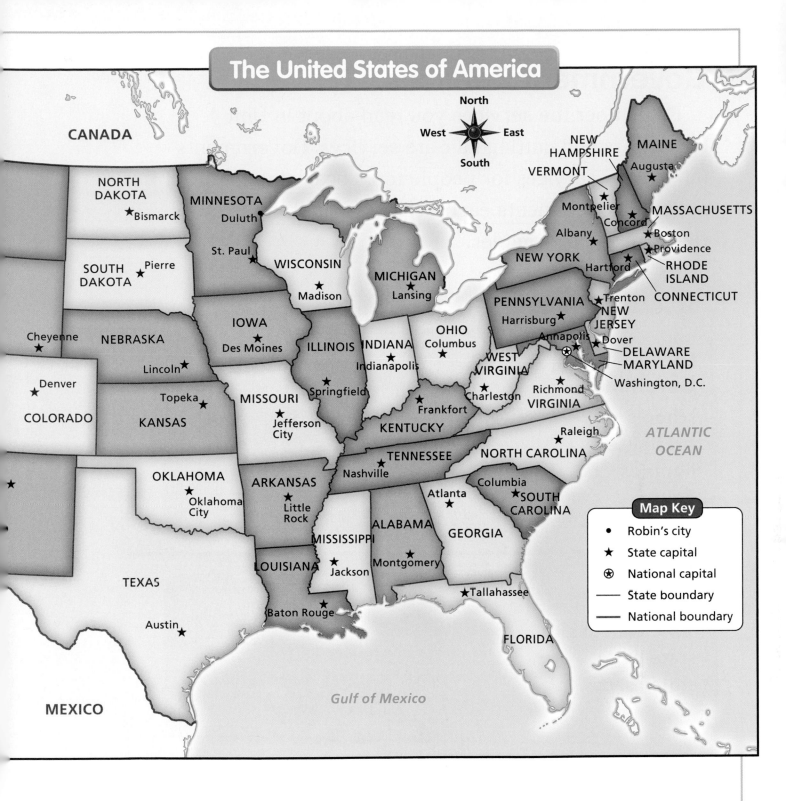

The United States of America

Map Key
- • Robin's city
- ★ State capital
- ⊛ National capital
- —— State boundary
- ━━ National boundary

CANADA

MEXICO

ATLANTIC OCEAN

Gulf of Mexico

North
West East
South

NORTH DAKOTA ★Bismarck

SOUTH DAKOTA ★Pierre

MINNESOTA Duluth• St. Paul★

WISCONSIN ★Madison

MICHIGAN Lansing★

MAINE Augusta★

NEW HAMPSHIRE ★Montpelier

VERMONT Concord★

MASSACHUSETTS ★Boston

NEW YORK Albany★ Hartford★ Providence★

RHODE ISLAND

CONNECTICUT

PENNSYLVANIA Harrisburg★ Trenton★

NEW JERSEY Dover★

DELAWARE

MARYLAND Annapolis★

Washington, D.C.⊛

IOWA Des Moines★

NEBRASKA Lincoln★

Cheyenne★

Denver★

COLORADO

KANSAS Topeka★

ILLINOIS Springfield★

MISSOURI Jefferson City★

INDIANA Indianapolis★

OHIO Columbus★

WEST VIRGINIA Charleston★

VIRGINIA Richmond★

KENTUCKY Frankfort★

TENNESSEE Nashville★

NORTH CAROLINA Raleigh★

OKLAHOMA Oklahoma City★

ARKANSAS Little Rock★

MISSISSIPPI Jackson★

ALABAMA Montgomery★

GEORGIA Atlanta★

SOUTH CAROLINA Columbia★

LOUISIANA Baton Rouge★

TEXAS Austin★

FLORIDA Tallahassee★

Skill **Reading Maps** Find Duluth, Minnesota.
Is Duluth north, or south, of the state capital
of Minnesota?

Government Services

Remember the services you read about in Unit 4. Fixing cars and cutting hair are services. Governments have many services for people too. <u>Local, state, and national governments each help with different services.</u> Here are some examples.

(main ★ idea)

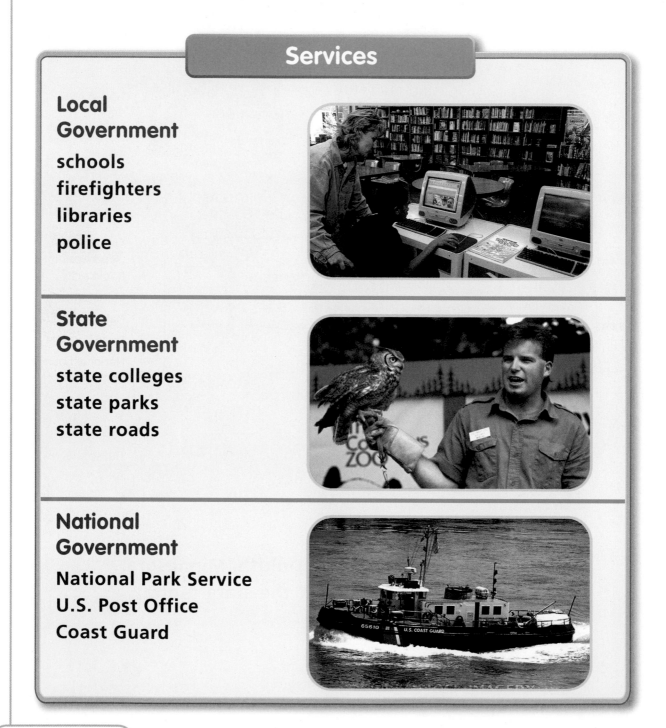

Services

Local Government

schools
firefighters
libraries
police

State Government

state colleges
state parks
state roads

National Government

National Park Service
U.S. Post Office
Coast Guard

Taxes

How do governments pay for services? Governments collect money called <u>taxes.</u> Workers pay income taxes from the money they earn. Businesses also pay income taxes. In most states, people pay sales taxes when they buy goods such as bikes or baseballs. Governments use money from taxes to pay for services such as parks, police, and roads.

main idea (★)

Review Why do governments need taxes?

	35.00
Baseball Bat	8.00
Baseball	40.00
Baseball glove	
	83.00
SUBTOTAL	3.32
Georgia Tax 4.00%	$86.32
TOTAL	
	90.00
Cash	3.68
Cash Change	

Lesson Review

❶ **Vocabulary** Write a sentence that explains what **taxes** are.

❷ **Main Idea** What are the three governments that people have?

Activity Write or tell about a local government service you use. Explain how it helps you and other people.

Fire Fighters

From **The Fire Station** by Stuart A. Kallen

When a fire alarm rings, fire fighters race into action. Fire fighters are men and women who risk their lives every day. Their most important job is to put out fires that threaten lives and property. They must learn how to do this at fire fighters' school.

Fire fighters drive long red fire trucks to help pump the water onto fires. Huge hoses shoot water onto fires. Fire fighters use ladders to climb into the windows of burning buildings. They use axes to break through burning doors and walls.

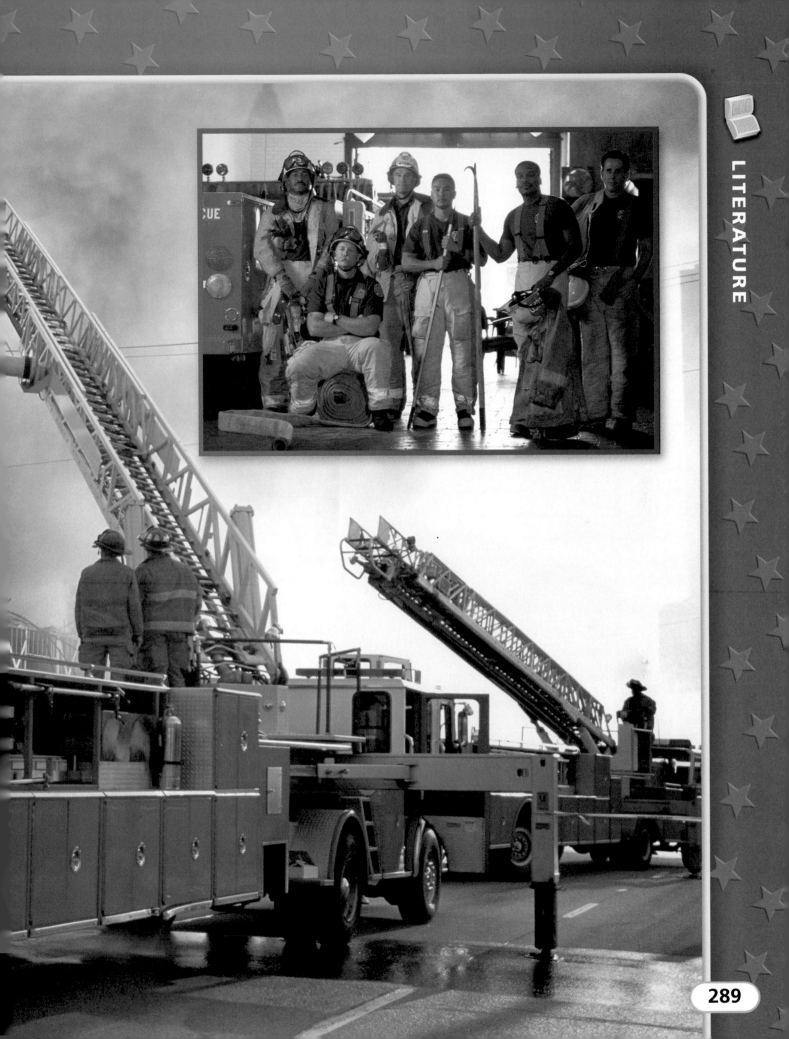

Fighting fires is hard, dangerous work. Sometimes fire fighters lose their lives in fires. Almost every city and town has a monument to fire fighters. Some are honored with medals and decorations.

Fire fighters don't just rescue people. They rescue dogs, cats and other pets.

You can be sure that if there is an emergency a firefighter will be there as soon as possible.

A fire fighter uses an extension ladder to get water to fires in skyscrapers.

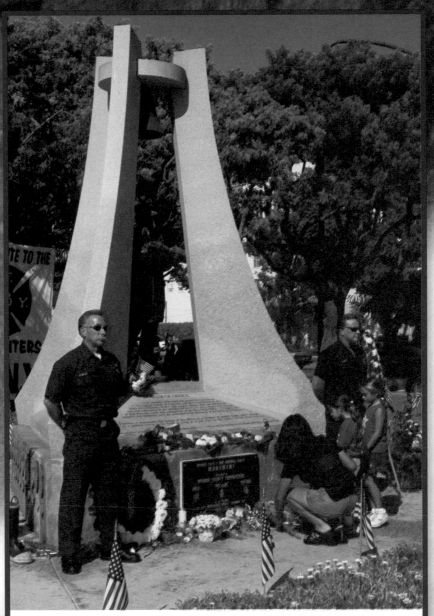

A fire fighters' memorial

Activities

1. **Talk About It** Draw a fire fighter at work. Tell about your drawing.

2. **Write About It** Write about how a fire fighter shows courage.

Citizens Make a Difference

Vocabulary

citizen
right
responsibility

Reading Skill

Classify

Build on What You Know

Think of ways students have made your school a good place to learn. You will read about how you are a citizen in your school, community, and nation.

You Are a Citizen

A **citizen** is a person who belongs to a place. You are a citizen of the community where you live and the nation where you were born. You can also become a citizen of the United States even if you were not born here.

main (★) idea

Citizens Have Rights

As a citizen, you have rights that the government protects. A **right** is something you may do. As a citizen of the United States, you have a right to speak freely and to practice your religion. You also have the right to privacy. That means you may decide what to show or tell someone and what not to tell.

Review What rights do you have as a citizen?

Citizens Have Responsibilities

Along with rights, citizens have responsibilities. A **responsibility** is something that you should do. A responsibility may be following rules or doing a chore. It may be treating others fairly. Name some responsibilities you have. What would happen if you did not do them?

main idea

Skill **Reading Visuals** What are the citizens doing for their community?

Being a Good Citizen

Good citizens care about people's rights. They try to make things fair and safe for everyone. Good citizens work together to solve problems. Children can be good citizens by solving problems together in their school or community. Look at the four steps.

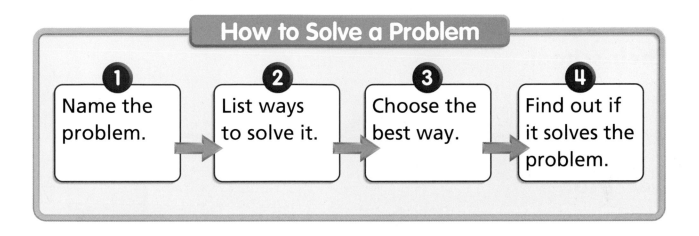

How to Solve a Problem

1 Name the problem.

2 List ways to solve it.

3 Choose the best way.

4 Find out if it solves the problem.

Review How can you be a good citizen?

Lesson Review

1 **Vocabulary** Name two **rights** of **citizens** in the United States.

2 **Main Idea** Copy this sentence. Fill in the blanks. Citizens of the United States have _____ and _____.

HANDS ON **Activity** Draw a poster that shows how to be a good citizen. Write sentences to explain your ideas.

Readers' Theater

Solving Problems

Read about some students who take **responsibility** to try to solve a problem at their school.

Narrator

Lisa: student

Greg: student

Mimi: student

Don: student

Mr. Vacca: teacher

Ms. Leroy: principal

Scene 1

Narrator: We are in Mr. Vacca's classroom. It's a Friday in May. Our class is almost ready to go home. Then the principal, Ms. Leroy, speaks on the intercom.

Ms. Leroy: Next week the builders will start the new addition to our school. They will have to take out all the bike racks. After that, no one can ride a bike to school.

Lisa: So we can't ride our bikes to school all spring!

Mr. Vacca: Everyone listen, please!

Ms. Leroy: Please make sure to take my letter home to your families. It tells why students cannot ride bikes to school.

Mr. Vacca: Now everyone may go, quietly! Have a good weekend.

Don: How can we have a good weekend with bad news like that?

Mimi: Maybe it will be good if we can solve the bike problem!

Lisa: Let's meet at the bike racks to talk about it.

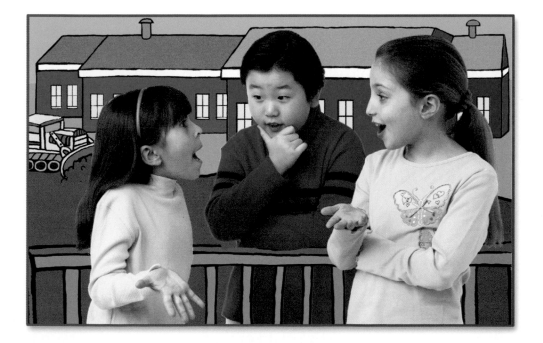

Scene 2

Narrator: Lisa, Greg, Mimi, and Don meet at the bike racks.

Lisa: First we have to name the problem.

Greg: The problem is we want to ride our bikes to school, but now we can't.

Lisa: Next we should name the reasons why we can't ride our bikes.

Greg: Because they're building where the bike racks are.

Mimi: Then let's tell them not to build!

Don: But we want them to build. They are building a theater and a new gym.

Mimi: What if we hid Ms. Leroy's letter from our families and rode our bikes anyway?

Lisa: That could only work for one day!

Don: And we would be in big trouble!

Greg: Here's another idea. Maybe they can move the bike racks to the other side of the school.

Lisa: That should work! Let's go talk to Ms. Leroy.

Don: I'll bet she'll listen. She likes kids to show responsibility. Maybe she can help us think of another way to solve the problem if our idea doesn't work.

Activities

1. **Think About It** Do you like the way the students tried to solve the problem? Why?

2. **Write About It** Write or tell what Ms. Leroy might say when the students talk to her.

Laws

▶ **Vocabulary**

law

judge

◎ **Reading Skill**

**Main Idea
and Details**

Build on What You Know

What are some rules in your school or classroom? Learn how they are like rules in a community, state, or country.

Laws Are Important

A **law** is a rule that everyone in a community, state, or country must follow. Laws keep people safe and help them get along with one another. What do you think would happen if there were no traffic laws?

*main
(★)
idea*

Review Why are laws important?

The signs on this page tell people about laws.

DO NOT FEED THE ANIMALS

SCHOOL ZONE

STOP

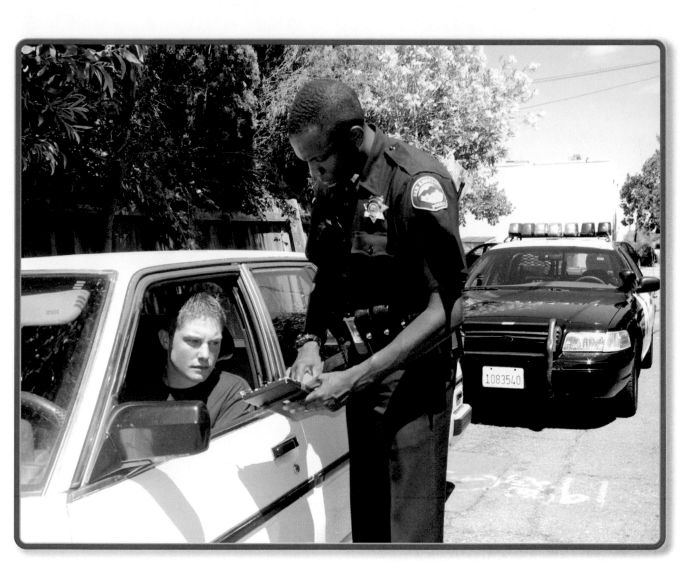

Police stop drivers who speed.

Police Help with Laws

Local, state, and national governments have laws. Police help with government laws. They tell people how to obey (oh BAY) laws. They stop people who break laws. Look at the picture on this page. What do you think is happening? Think of another way that police help with laws.

main idea (★)

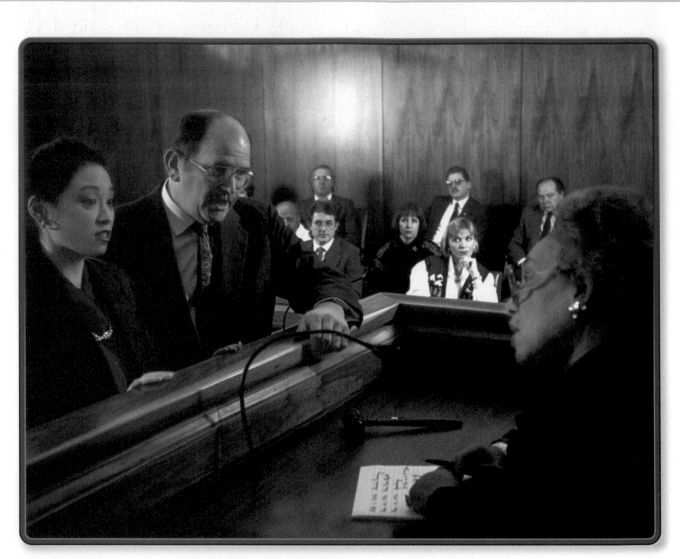

In Court Judges work in courts, where people come when they have problems with laws. Here two lawyers talk to a judge.

Judges Help with Laws

A judge is someone who helps decide when people don't agree about laws. Governments have many, many laws. Judges know the laws well. They help decide if someone has broken a law. Judges say what people must do to make up for breaking laws.

Citizens Help with Laws

Citizens protect each other when they know and follow laws. When people obey a traffic law, they help keep others safe. When you follow laws in a park, you help others enjoy the park. Citizens help by choosing good people to make laws. Also citizens can work together to make better laws.

main idea (★)

States have laws about driving. In many states, you must be sixteen before you can get a permit to learn to drive.

Review What can citizens do to help with laws?

Lesson Review

1. **Vocabulary** Tell two things that **judges** do.

2. **Main Idea** What would happen if drivers did not pay attention to traffic lights?

✏ **Activity** Name a law that you think is important. Write or tell why you think it is important.

Rosa Parks

Rosa Parks in 1999

Not everyone is brave enough to risk jail for what they believe is right. In 1955, Rosa Parks showed courage when she stood up for her beliefs.

At that time Rosa Parks was living in Montgomery, Alabama. The state's **laws** and rules did not give African American people the same rights as white people. This seemed very wrong to Rosa Parks. She began to work with others who wanted fair laws and rights for everyone.

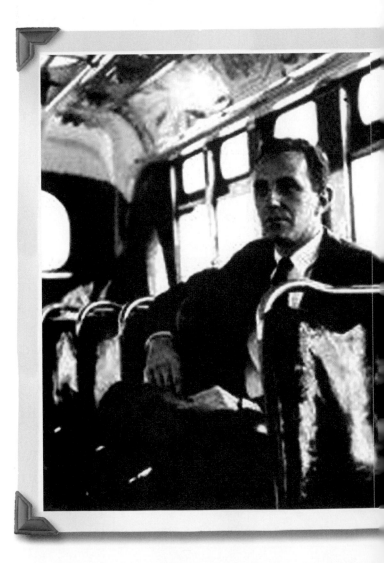

Rosa Parks helped change a law that was unfair to African American people on buses.

Taking Action

On December 1, 1955, Rosa Parks acted against an unfair law. The law made African Americans give up their bus seats to white people.

Rosa Parks stayed firmly in her seat when the bus driver tried to make her give it up. For this she had to go to jail. Her action led many others to work together to change the unfair law.

Activities

1. **Talk About It** How did Rosa Parks show courage?

2. **Build It** Make a mobile that shows pictures of citizens who did something brave.

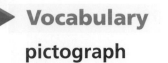

Read a Pictograph

► **Vocabulary**

pictograph

A school started a project to recycle cans. The children used a pictograph to keep track of the cans they collected.

Learn the Skill

A **pictograph** is a way to compare things. A pictograph uses pictures to show numbers of things.

Step 1 Look at the title. It tells what the pictograph is about.

Step 2 Look at the key. It shows what each picture of a can stands for.

Step 3 Count the cans for Class A. There are seven cans. So Class A collected seven 10s, or seventy, cans.

Practice the Skill

Look at the graph below. Then follow the directions.

1 What is the title of this pictograph?

2 How many cans did Class C collect?

3 How many cans did Class E collect?

4 How many cans did Classes B and D collect together?

Key

= 10 cans

Number of Cans Collected

| Class A | Class B | Class C | Class D | Class E |

Vocabulary

vote
election
ballot

Reading Skill

Sequence

Leaders

Build on What You Know

Sports teams and school bands have leaders. What are some other kinds of leaders? Governments have leaders too.

Choosing Leaders

Did you ever choose a leader for a team? When you show or write a choice, you **vote.** Your school might have an **election,** which is a time when people vote. When you turn eighteen, you will have the right to vote in government elections. You may vote for many different leaders in one election. The chart shows three examples.

main idea

Government Leaders

Local Government

Citizens may vote for mayor of their city or town.

State Government

Citizens may vote for governor of the state where they live.

National Government

Citizens may vote for President of the United States.

Government leaders have important jobs. Some make laws. Others make sure the laws work well. In elections, citizens get to choose leaders who they think can do these jobs the best.

main idea

Review Why should citizens vote in government elections?

Before You Vote

What can citizens do to choose the best leaders? They can read newspapers and watch television. They can ask questions of leaders. They can ask themselves questions.

Will you add more bus stops?

What can you do to fix our playgrounds?

My Questions

★ Are leaders honest and smart?   YES

★ Will leaders work hard for all citizens?   YES

★ Can leaders run the government best?   YES

Leaders and Citizens

A **ballot** is a form on which people mark their choices. In elections, citizens vote on ballots.

Leaders who win elections need to keep listening to citizens. Citizens need to keep telling leaders what they want for their community, state, and country. Citizens and leaders together help governments work well.

main idea (★)

People who run for election explain how they will work for citizens.

Review Why should leaders talk with citizens?

Lesson Review

1 **Vocabulary** Use the words **vote** and **election** to tell some things you know about leaders.

2 **Main Idea** Tell something that government leaders do.

Activity Write or tell two things a voter can do before an election.

Voting with Ballots

The eagle is a symbol for our national government. You can choose an animal to be a symbol for your class. Think of animals that stand for something you feel proud about, such as being kind or smart.

Choose between the two animals you see on the box, or decide on two different animals to choose from. Have an election in your classroom. Use a ballot to mark your choice. Then count the votes to know the winning symbol for your class.

Look at the two animals. Think about their special features. Decide which is the best symbol for your class. Make speeches and signs.

❷ Mark your ballot with your choice. Do not write your name on your ballot! It's a secret vote. Add your ballot to a big box.

❸ Help count the votes for each animal. Write down the totals. Check your counts and totals. Which symbol won? Plan together how to show your new class symbol.

Skillbuilder

Resolve a Conflict

▶ **Vocabulary**

conflict

People in classrooms and communities don't always agree. When people disagree, it is called a **conflict.** Together, people can resolve conflicts.

Learn the Skill

Follow the steps to help resolve a conflict.

Step 1 Look at the picture. Describe the conflict. Two children want to use the computer at the same time.

Step 2 Think about what each child wants to do.

 Write   Play Games

Step 3 Think of ways to resolve the conflict.

- Take turns.
- Writer uses pencil.
- Game player plays board game.

Step 4 Ask yourself about each idea: Can both children do some of what they want? Choose the best way to resolve the conflict.

Practice the Skill

Work with a small group. Look at the picture below. Then follow the directions.

1 Tell in your own words what the conflict is. What does each group want?

2 List some ways to resolve the conflict.

3 Choose the best solution. Tell why your solution is the best one.

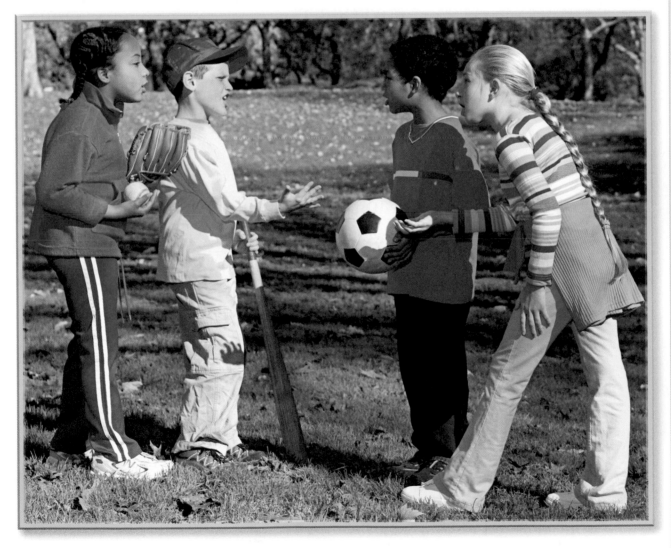

National Government

Build on What You Know

When you start a class project, you may write a plan for how it will work. In a way, that is like the plan that early leaders wrote for our nation's government.

Vocabulary

Constitution
democracy
liberty
justice

Reading Skill

Classify

A Plan for Government

In Unit 5 you read about the Revolutionary War. When that war ended, American leaders did not want a king to rule the new nation. The leaders met and wrote a new plan for the government. That plan is called the **Constitution.**

Review What is the Constitution?

Skill **Visual Learning** Leaders worked on the Constitution in Philadelphia in 1787. What do you notice about their clothes and hair?

Important Words

The writers of the Constitution planned a **democracy,** which is government by the people. They used words that they believed were important in a democracy. One word was **liberty,** which means "freedom." Another was **justice,** which means "fairness." Why are they still important words today?

Government in Three Parts

The Constitution is more than 200 years old. It is still the plan for our government today. <u>The Constitution describes a government in three parts, or branches.</u> Each branch has its own building in Washington, D.C. On these pages you can read about the people who work in those buildings.

(★) main idea

Review How many branches does the government have?

White House

The President of the United States is the leader of the nation. The President lives and works in the White House.

Capitol

The members of Congress make laws. Men and women in Congress come from all fifty states. They work in the Capitol Building.

Supreme Court

The Supreme Court has nine judges who look carefully at laws. They decide if the laws are fair and protect citizens' rights. They meet in the Supreme Court Building.

Lesson Review

❶ **Vocabulary** When do you say, "with liberty and justice for all"? Tell what it means.

❷ **Main Idea** What are the three branches of the national government?

HANDS ON

Activity Make a chart that shows who works in the three branches of government.

Democracy

Democracy is government that comes from the people. In a democracy, people make choices about their leaders and their laws. They may do this by voting in an election.

In the United States, citizens may vote for a leader of their community or state. They may also vote for a few people from their state to go to Washington, D.C. Those people are members of Congress. In Congress, they vote to make laws for all citizens in the country. Look at examples of democracy in the United States.

School

Students vote on where to have their class picnic.

Community

This city council votes on how much money to spend on city services.

Democracy in Action

Nation

People vote for a new President of the United States.

State

People hear a speech before they vote for governor.

Activities

1. **Talk About It** Tell how democracy is part of what happens in your class or school.

2. **Write About It** Write about why voting is important in a democracy.

Our Nation and the World

Build on What You Know

Have you ever worked with a friend to solve a problem? Sometimes nations work together to try to solve problems.

Vocabulary
aid

Reading Skill
Problem and Solution

Nations Help Each Other

The United States is one of more than two hundred nations in the world. Nations sometime work out ways to help each other. If storms destroy crops in one nation, other nations may send aid. **Aid** is help. It can be money, goods, or services. What goods or services might people need after a big storm?

main idea (★)

U.S. troops give bags of food to people in Honduras after a hurricane.

United States President Jimmy Carter sits between President Anwar el-Sadat of Egypt (left) and Prime Minister Menachem Begin of Israel after the signing of a peace treaty between Israel and Egypt.

Leaders Work Together

Every nation has a government. Government leaders from different nations work together. They talk about how to make the earth cleaner and safer. Leaders have meetings about trade, health, and peace. Government leaders travel to visit each other. They stay in touch by phone, mail, and the Internet.

Review Why do leaders from different countries work together?

Meetings Around the World

Here are a few places where world leaders have met to discuss problems.

United States, Washington, D.C.

Beijing, CHINA

SOUTH AFRICA, Johannesburg

United States

President George W. Bush met in Washington, D.C. with President Vladimir Putin from Russia.

China

Jiang Zemin, the president of China (left) met with Prime Minister Tony Blair of Great Britain in Beijing.

South Africa

Palestinian leader Yasir Arafat met with President Nelson Mandela of South Africa in Johannesburg.

Review Why are meetings with leaders from different countries important?

Lesson Review

❶ Vocabulary Give an example of government **aid.**

❷ Main Idea What are two ways that government leaders from different countries stay in touch?

Activity Choose a leader whose country is not shown on the map on page 324. Find his or her country on a world map.

Flags of Different Nations

Did you know that there are more than 200 nations in the world? Every one of them has a different flag.

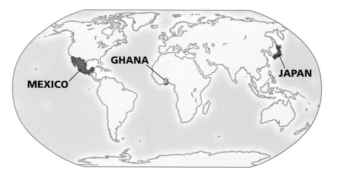

I live in **Mexico**. The eagle holding a snake is important in a legend of our country. Red, white, and green stand for our independence.

I live in **Japan**. The word Japan means "land of the rising sun." The red circle is the rising sun. It has been a symbol of my country for a very long time.

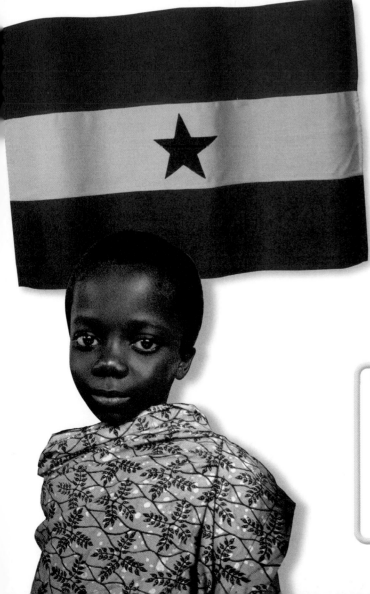

I live in **Ghana** in Africa. The black star on our flag is a symbol of freedom. The stripes have colors that are important in the flags of many African nations.

Activities

1. **Talk About It** What is one way that the three flags are alike?

2. **Write About It** Write something you learned about one of the three flags.

327

A Citizen's Government

Citizen

Local → City Hall

State → State Capitol

National → U.S. Capitol Building

Fill in three missing words that help describe the chart.

Each citizen has **1.** _____ , **2.** _____ , and **3.** _____ governments.

(page 284)

Facts and Main Ideas

4. Why do governments collect taxes? (page 287)

5. What is one responsibility that citizens have? (page 294)

6. What are two things citizens can do to choose good leaders? (page 310)

7. What is the Constitution? (page 316)

Vocabulary

Write the letter of the correct answer.

8. The money that people pay to a government

9. A person who belongs to a place

10. A freedom that government must protect

11. A time when people vote

> A. **right** (page 293)
>
> B. **election** (page 308)
>
> C. **taxes** (page 287)
>
> D. **citizen** (page 292)
>
> E. **judge** (page 302)

✔ Test Practice

12. What does the word **government** mean?

    A. A person who belongs to a place, such as a state

    B. A group of people who make and carry out laws

    C. A leader of a community, state, or country

    D. Something that people should do for others

Critical Thinking

Compare and Contrast

13. What are some ways that your local government is like your national government?

14. What are some ways that your local government is different from your national government?

Read a Pictograph

Mrs. Tan's class is choosing a place for a field trip. The pictograph shows the class's votes.

Votes for Our Field Trip

Aquarium	✔✔✔✔✔✔
Fire Station	✔✔✔
Bakery	✔✔✔✔
Dairy Farm	✔✔✔✔✔✔

15. Which choice has the most votes?

16. Which has the fewest?

17. How many children voted?

Resolve a Conflict

Jack, Lena, Darryl, and Kay all want another slice of pizza. There are only 2 slices of pizza left.

18. Choose the best way to resolve the conflict.

A   B   C

Make Up a Riddle

Think of a person, place, or thing you learned about in this unit. You might choose a government leader or service worker. Keep your choice secret.

❶ Fold a sheet of paper in half and write two riddle clues on the outside. Write your secret answer inside.

MY Clues
1. a plan
2. rights

❷ Show your clues to others. Can they guess?

Weekly Reader Project

Go to the Weekly Reader Website for directions to complete the **Government in the News** big book.

Government in the News

Technology
Current Events Project
For more activities and resources visit:
www.eduplace.com/kids/hmss05

In Your Classroom

Look for these Social Studies Independent Books in your classroom.

WELCOME TO THE WHITE HOUSE
by Jim Smith

What Does a GOVERNOR Do?
by Melissa Blackwell Burke

SUSAN B. ANTHONY
Fighter for Women's Rights
by Becky Ward

At the Library

You may find these books at your school or public library.

We the Kids
by David Catrow

City Green
by DyAnne DiSalvo-Ryan

Martin Luther King, Jr. Day

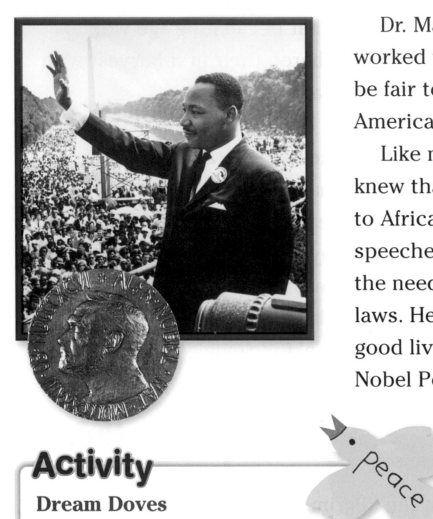

Dr. Martin Luther King, Jr., worked to make laws that would be fair to all people. Each year, Americans honor his work.

Like many people, Dr. King knew that some laws were not fair to African Americans. He gave speeches and marched to show the need to change the unfair laws. He shared his dream of good lives for all. He received the Nobel Peace Prize for his work.

Activity

Dream Doves

1. Think of a dream that you believe is good for everyone.

2. Write your dream on the shape of a dove.

peace

friendship

happiness

Presidents' Day

On Presidents' Day, people honor two important Presidents of the United States.

George Washington helped make the United States a free country. He led the army for the new country in the American Revolution. He was the first President of the United States.

Abraham Lincoln was another great President.

He helped to make all people in the United States equal and free. Lincoln helped keep the states together in one country.

Activity

"If I Am President" Poster

1. Think about what you would do if you were the President of the United States.

2. Make a poster to show your ideas.

Jenny for President!!!
I will:
plant trees
clean up trash
give children books

Memorial Day

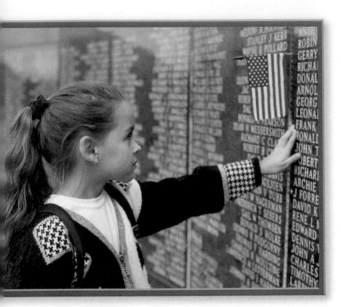

Vietnam Veterans Memorial

On Memorial Day, citizens of the United States remember the people who fought and died in wars.

A memorial is something that helps people remember a person, a group, or an event from the past. A memorial can be a statue, a sign, or a building. On Memorial Day, people gather at memorials and cemeteries.

People put flowers and flags on memorials and graves. Towns and cities have parades or speeches. Citizens honor the people who fought for the United States.

Activity

Make a Memorial Circle

1. Think of a person or an event you want to remember.

2. Write the words on a circle of colored paper. You may add a picture.

In memory of my grandpa Ted Barrios

In memory of people who fought in all wars

Flag Day

The United States flag stands for our country. On Flag Day, many communities have parades and sing the national anthem.

Our country's first flag had only 13 stripes and 13 stars. They stood for the 13 colonies that formed our country. Later the colonies became states.

Now there are 50 states in the United States. The United States flag has 50 stars that stand for our 50 states. It still has 13 stripes.

Activity

State Stars

1. Cut out the shape of a white star.

2. Write the name of a state in red. Write the capital of the state in blue.

Independence Day

On the Fourth of July, we celebrate our country's birthday.

The United States was born on July 4, 1776. On that day, our leaders signed an important paper. It said that our land and our people were now free from Great Britain.

Independence is another word for **freedom**. Every Fourth of July, we celebrate our country's freedom. Towns and cities have parades and picnics. Many communities have fireworks at night.

Activity

Freedom Poem

1. Think of some things that United States citizens are free to do.

2. Write a poem about your freedoms. You may start with the words "I am free. . . ."

I am free to read books and talk to people.

I am free to think and learn.

I am free to be me!

References

Citizenship Handbook

Resources

Our Flag

Pledge of Allegiance

I **pledge allegiance** to the flag
of the United States of America
and to the **Republic** for which it stands,
one Nation under God, **indivisible,**
with **liberty** and **justice** for all.

**What does the Pledge of Allegiance mean?
Use the vocabulary to explain.**

pledge: promise
republic: nation
liberty: freedom
allegiance: loyalty
indivisible: cannot be divided
justice: fairness

Rules about the Flag

Look at some rules about our national flag. They come from a law called the United States Flag Code.

 The flag should have thirteen stripes, red and white. It should have white stars on a blue background. It should have a star for each state.

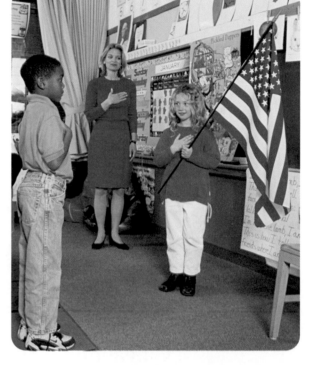

To salute the flag, stand straight and face the flag. Put your right hand on your heart.

Say the pledge while you salute.

Do not let the flag touch the ground.

Fly the United States flag above any state flag.

At night, take down the flag or light it up.

Songs of Our Nation

On page 143, you can read the words to "The Star-Spangled Banner," our national anthem. Many other songs also show our pride in our country. How did they come to be?

In 1893, a teacher from the East named Katharine Lee Bates took a trip to the West. The beauty of mountains, plains, and open skies inspired her to write a poem. Bates's poem became the words for the song "America the Beautiful."

"America the Beautiful"

by Katharine Lee Bates

O beautiful for spacious skies,
    For amber waves of grain,
For purple mountain majesties
    Above the fruited plain.
America! America!
    God shed His grace on thee
And crown thy good with brotherhood
    From sea to shining sea.

Vocabulary

spacious: spread over a large area

amber: golden brown

majesties: powers

fruited: successfully planted

shed: give out

grace: blessing

thee: you

brotherhood: friendship

What does the song mean to you?
The words above help explain the song.

Samuel F. Smith heard the British national anthem in 1832 and liked the music. He wrote words so that Americans could sing it. "America," or "My Country, 'Tis of Thee," quickly became a favorite of many people in the United States. People still love to sing it today.

"America"

by Samuel F. Smith

My country, 'tis of thee,

Sweet land of liberty,

  Of thee I sing;

Land where my fathers died,

Land of the Pilgrims' pride,

From every mountain-side

  Let freedom ring.

Irving Berlin first wrote "God Bless America" for a show in 1918 but did not use it then. Twenty years later, when it seemed that war would break out at any minute, he decided to revise the song. Kate Smith, a famous singer, sang it on a radio program. People loved the song, and it has been an American favorite ever since.

"God Bless America"

by Irving Berlin

God bless America,

Land that I love,

Stand beside her and guide her

Through the night with a light from above.

From the mountains, to the prairies,

To the oceans white with foam,

God bless America,

My home sweet home.

Character Traits

A character trait is something people show by the way they act. A person who acts bravely shows courage, and courage is a character trait.

Character traits are also called "life skills." Life skills can help you do your best, and doing your best leads to reaching your goals.

Rosa Parks
Courage
Rosa Parks showed courage by acting against an unfair law.

Paul Revere
Patriotism
Paul Revere showed patriotism by riding to warn the colonists about the plans of the British army.

Courage means acting bravely. It takes courage to be honest and tell the truth.

Patriotism is being proud of your country and working for your country's goals.

Responsibility means doing all your work. You can count on people who show responsibility. They will do all the things they are asked to do.

Respect means paying attention to what other people want and believe. Treating others with respect helps everyone get along.

Fairness means acting to make things fair for everyone.

Civic virtue is good citizenship. It means doing things to help communities live and work well together.

Caring is helping others. Listening to how other people feel is also caring.

Geographic Terms

forest
a large area of land where many trees grow

hill
a raised mass of land, smaller than a mountain

▲ **desert**
a dry area where few plants grow

▲ **island**
land with water all around it

lake
a body of water with land all around it

mountains

hill

river

lake

ocean

mountain
a steep mass of land, much higher than the surrounding country

▲ **ocean**
a salty body of water covering a large area of the earth

peninsula
land that sticks out into water

plain
a broad, flat area of land

plateau
an area of flat land that is higher than the land around it

river
a large stream of water that runs into a lake, ocean, or another river

valley
low land between mountains or hills

valley

peninsula

plain

Atlas

ARCTIC OCEAN

NORTH
AMERICA

UNITED STATES

PACIFIC
OCEAN

ATLANTIC
OCEAN

Equator

SOUTH
AMERICA

ATLANTIC
OCEAN

PACIFIC
OCEAN

Atlas

ARCTIC OCEAN

EUROPE

ASIA

PACIFIC
OCEAN

AFRICA

Equator

INDIAN
OCEAN

AUSTRALIA

North

West — East

South

Scale at Equator

0   1,000   2,000 kilometers

0   1,000   2,000 miles

ANTARCTICA

The World: Physical

ARCTIC OCEAN

Mt. McKinley

ROCKY MOUNTAINS

Mississippi River

PACIFIC
OCEAN

ATLANTIC
OCEAN

Equator

Amazon River

A
N
D
E
S

PACIFIC
OCEAN

ATLANTIC
OCEAN

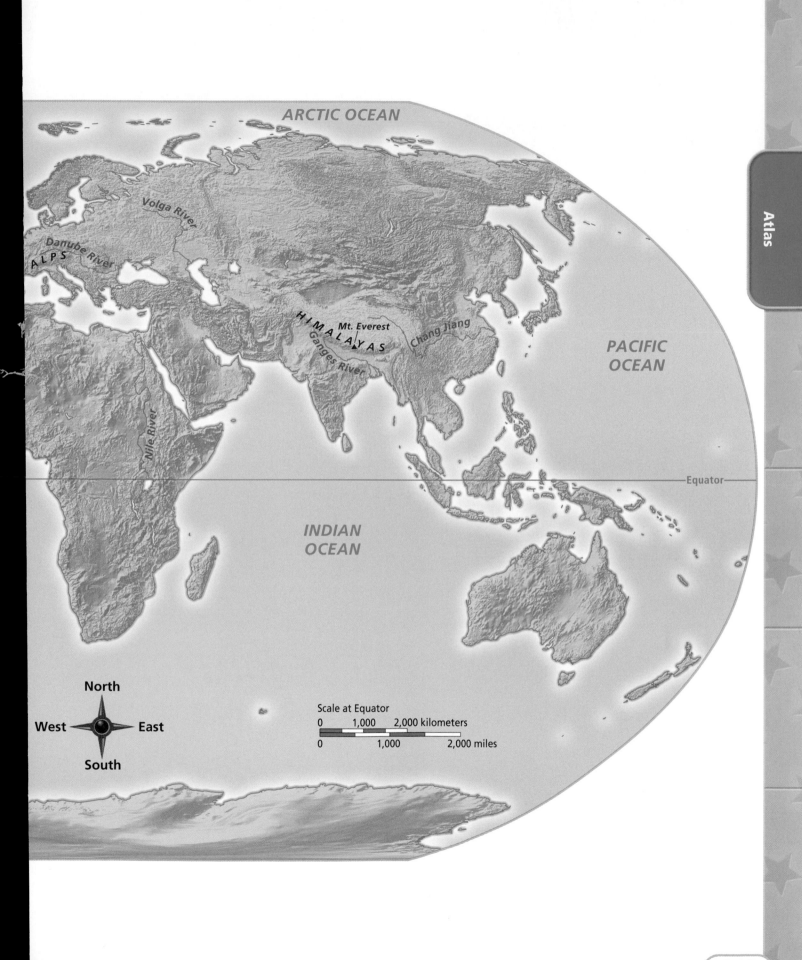

ARCTIC OCEAN

Volga River

Danube River

ALPS

Nile River

HIMALAYAS
Mt. Everest
Ganges River
Chang Jiang

PACIFIC OCEAN

Equator

INDIAN OCEAN

North

West — East

South

Scale at Equator
0   1,000   2,000 kilometers
0   1,000   2,000 miles

Canada, United States, Mexico

North

West ⟡ East

South

PACIFIC OCEAN

Map Key

⊛ National Capital

— National Boundary

| 0 | 400 | 800 kilometers |
| 0 | 400 | 800 miles |

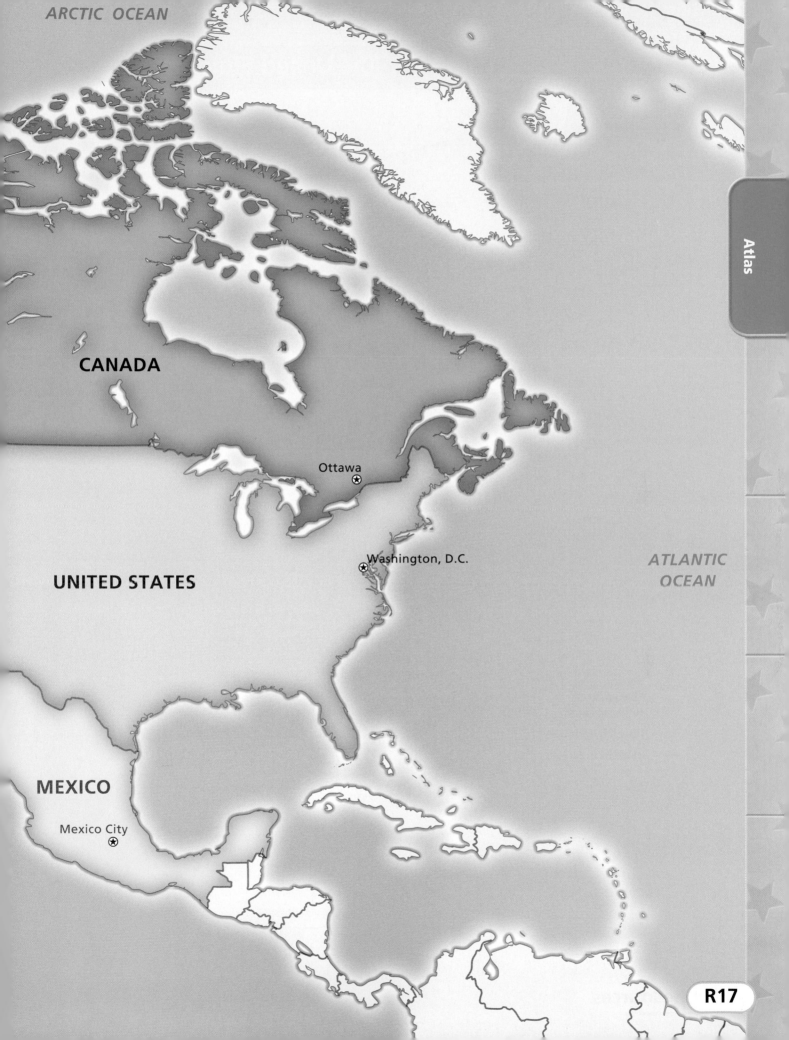

ARCTIC OCEAN

CANADA

UNITED STATES

Ottawa
⊛

Washington, D.C.
⊛

ATLANTIC
OCEAN

MEXICO

Mexico City
⊛

The United States

ALASKA

0 500 kilometers
0 500 miles

WASHINGTON

MONTANA

OREGON

IDAHO

North

West — East

South

NEVADA

WYOMING

UTAH

COLORADO

CALIFORNIA

ARIZONA

NEW
MEXICO

Map Key

⊛ National Capital

—— National Boundary

—— State Boundary

HAWAII

0 200 kilometers
0 200 miles

NEW
HAMPSHIRE

VERMONT

MAINE

MASSACHUSETTS

NEW
YORK

RHODE
ISLAND

CONNECTICUT

PENNSYLVANIA

NEW
JERSEY

DELAWARE

Washington, D.C.

MARYLAND

NORTH
DAKOTA

MINNESOTA

SOUTH
DAKOTA

WISCONSIN

MICHIGAN

IOWA

OHIO

WEST
VIRGINIA

VIRGINIA

NEBRASKA

ILLINOIS

INDIANA

KANSAS

MISSOURI

KENTUCKY

NORTH
CAROLINA

TENNESSEE

OKLAHOMA

ARKANSAS

SOUTH
CAROLINA

ALABAMA

GEORGIA

MISSISSIPPI

TEXAS

LOUISIANA

FLORIDA

0   125   250 kilometers

0   125   250 miles

Picture Glossary

A

aid

Help to others is a kind of **aid**. (p. 322) The United States often sends **aid** to countries where an earthquake has struck.

ancestor

A family member who lived before you is an **ancestor.** (p. 120) An **ancestor** of mine lived in China in the 1600s.

B

ballot

A **ballot** is a form on which people mark their choices in an election. (p. 311) Many communities have switched from paper **ballots** to voting machines.

bank

A **bank** is a safe place to keep money. (p. 181) Dad went to the **bank** to get money for gas.

bar graph

A **bar graph** is a chart that uses bars to show amounts. (p. 178) The **bar graph** shows the number of different workers in a school.

Number of Workers in Our School

Cafeteria Classrooms Office Media center

barter

The exchange of goods or services without the use of money is called **barter.** (p. 196) **Barter** takes place when you swap goods or services with someone.

calendar

A **calendar** is a chart that shows the months, weeks, and days of the year. (p. 50) I marked my birthday on the **calendar.**

capital

A **capital** is a city where the people in a government work. (p. 284) The **capital** of New Jersey is Trenton.

capital resource

Something other than natural or human resources, that people need in order to produce goods is a **capital resource.** (p. 191) **Capital resources** include tools, machinery, buildings, and trucks.

cause

A **cause** is something that makes something else happen. (p. 238) The **cause** of the fire was a lightning strike.

citizen

A **citizen** is a person who belongs to a place. (p. 292) You are a **citizen** of the community where you live.

climate

The usual weather of a place over a long time is called **climate.** (p. 85) Southern Michigan has a **climate** with cold winters and warm summers.

colonist

A **colonist** is a person who lives in a colony. (p. 230) The **colonists** at Jamestown came from England.

colony

A **colony** is a place that is ruled by another country. (p. 229) England's first **colony** in North America was Jamestown.

communication

Any way of sharing information is **communication.** (p. 268) Newspapers and magazines are kinds of **communication.**

community

A **community** is a place where people live. (p. 38) Cities and towns are **communities.**

compass rose

A **compass rose** is a drawing that shows directions on a map. (p. 34) Use the **compass rose** to find north.

conflict

A **conflict** is a disagreement. (p. 314) Good citizens try to resolve **conflicts** peacefully.

Constitution

The **Constitution** is a plan for the government of he United States. (p. 316) The United States **Constitution** is more than 200 years old.

consumer

A **consumer** is someone who buys or uses goods or services. (p. 166) I am a **consumer** when I buy food at a store.

continent

A **continent** is a large body of land. (p. 68) The earth has seven **continents.**

country

A **country** is a land where people have the same laws and leaders. (p. 67) Mexico is the **country** south of the United States.

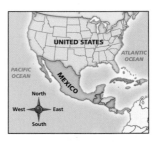

culture

The way of life of a group of people is called **culture.** (p. 117) Religious beliefs are part of people's **culture.**

custom

A **custom** is something that people usually do at a certain time. (p. 116) It is our **custom** to wear party hats at birthday parties.

decision

A **decision** is the act of deciding or of making a choice. (p. 150) I had to make a **decision** about doing my homework before or after supper.

democracy

A **democracy** is government by the people. (p. 317) People in a **democracy** choose their leaders.

detail

A **detail** is a small piece of information. (p. 98) Make sure you support your idea with **details.**

Main Idea
Details
1.
2.
3.
4.
5.

dictionary

A **dictionary** is a book that gives the meanings of words. (p. 186) Look up new words in a **dictionary.**

distance

The word **distance** means how far one point is from another. (p. 202) The **distance** across the table is 30 inches.

effect

An **effect** is something that happens as a result of a cause. (p. 238) An **effect** of playing in puddles is wet clothing.

cause	→	effect

election

An **election** is a time when people vote. (p. 308) We have an **election** to choose a new President every four years.

encyclopedia

An **encyclopedia** is a book or set of books that gives information about many topics. (p. 186) Look up a topic in an **encyclopedia** to find out more about it.

environment

The **environment** is the natural world around you. (p. 103) Land, water, plants, animals, and people are all part of the **environment.**

equator

The **equator** is an imaginary line that divides the earth into its northern and southern halves. (p. 72) You can only see the **equator** on maps.

explorer

An **explorer** is a person who travels to find new things and places. (p. 222) Columbus was an **explorer** who traveled to the Americas.

fact

A **fact** is something that is true. (pp. 164, 250) A book about seashells has many **facts** in it.

factory

A **factory** is a place where goods are made. (p. 172) It would be fun to go to a sneaker **factory.**

fiction

Written works that tell about made-up events and characters are called **fiction.** (p. 164) The stories "Cinderella" and **Sheep Out to Eat** are **fiction.**

globe

A **globe** is a ball-shaped model of the earth. (p. 32) A **globe** shows the true shape of the earth.

goods

Things people make or grow are called **goods.** (p. 172) Goods are things such as trucks and apples.

government

A group of people who work together to run a community, state, or country make up a **government.** (p. 283) Some people in our **government** work at city hall.

grid

A **grid** is a pattern of lines that form boxes. (p. 42) A **grid** helps you find places on a map.

group

A **group** is a number of people who live together, work together, or spend time together. (p. 26) A soccer team is a **group.**

hemisphere

A **hemisphere** is half the earth. (p. 72) North America is in the Western **Hemisphere.**

hero

A **hero** is someone who is admired for great courage or for doing something important. (p. 252) **Heroes** can be found in medicine, sports, science, or other areas.

history

Everything people can know about the past is called **history.** (p. 212) The invention of the computer was an important event in **history.**

human resource

A **human resource** is a person who helps make a product. (p. 190) A worker in a factory or other places is a **human resource.**

immigrant

An **immigrant** is a person who moves from one country to another. (p. 118) In the 1970s, many **immigrants** came to the United States from Asia.

income

The money people earn when they work is called **income.** (p. 168) My mother uses her **income** to pay for our food.

independence

Independence means freedom from the rule of another nation. (p. 242) The 13 colonies wanted **independence** from Britain.

interview

An **interview** is a meeting in which one person asks another person questions. (p. 134) In our **interview** with the mayor, we asked five questions.

invention

An **invention** is something new that someone makes or thinks of. (p. 256) Thomas Edison thought of many important **inventions.**

island

An **island** is a piece of land with water all around it. (p. 76) Greenland is a very large **island.**

journey

A **journey** is a long trip. (p. 222) Colonists from England made a **journey** from Europe to North America.

judge

A **judge** is someone who studies the

laws and decides the best way to follow them. (p. 302) A **judge** may decide what a person must do to make up for breaking a law.

justice

Justice means fairness. (p. 317) A good judge treats everyone with **justice.**

lake

A body of water with land all around it is

called a **lake.** (p. 78) Most **lakes** have fresh water.

landform

A **landform** is one of the shapes of land found on

the earth. (p. 74) A mountain is a **landform.**

landmark

A **landmark** is something that helps people know a place. (p. 138) The Gateway Arch is a **landmark** of St. Louis, Missouri.

law

A rule that everyone in a community,

state, or nation must follow is called a **law.** (p. 300) A driver who doesn't stop at a stop sign is breaking a **law.**

leader

A **leader** is someone who leads others. (p. 28) A community **leader** guides the work of others.

legend

A **legend** is a story that people have passed along for many years. (p. 128) Most cultures have a **legend** that explains weather.

liberty

The word **liberty** means freedom. (p. 317) The **Liberty** Bell is a symbol of our nation's freedom.

location

A **location** is a place. (p. 42) An airplane symbol may mark the **location** of an airport on a map.

main idea

The most important thought on a page is called a **main idea.** (p. 98) The **main idea** on that page is that people have many kinds of pets.

market

A **market** is any place where people buy and sell things. (p. 55) A small store is one kind of **market.**

memorial

A **memorial** is something, such as a building or statue, that honors a hero or an event. (p. 140) The Vietnam Veterans **Memorial** honors Americans who were killed in the Vietnam War.

monument

A **monument** is something, such as a building or statue, that honors a hero or an event. (p. 140) Many towns have a **monument** to people who served in a war.

nation

Nation is another word for country. (p. 69) Canada is a **nation** to the north of the United States.

national holiday

A **national holiday** is a holiday that honors someone or something that is important to a country. (p. 144) Independence Day is a **national holiday** that honors the beginning of the United States.

natural resource

Something in nature that people use is a **natural resource.** (p. 100) Water is an important **natural resource.**

needs

Things that people must have to live are called **needs.** (p. 160) Our **needs** are food, water, clothing, and shelter.

neighborhood

A neighborhood is a part of a city or town. (p. 36) Each year, people in my **neighborhood** get together for a picnic on Labor Day.

nonfiction

Written materials that are about true things are **nonfiction.** (p. 164) **Sheep on the Farm** is a **nonfiction** book.

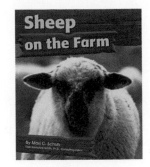

northeast

The direction between north and east is called **northeast.** (p. 82) New York City is **northeast** of Trenton, New Jersey.

northwest

The direction between north and west is called **northwest.** (p. 82) Montgomery, Alabama is **northwest** of Tallahassee, Florida.

opinion

An **opinion** is a belief based on what you think or feel, rather than on facts. (p. 250) In my **opinion** soccer is better than baseball.

peninsula

Land that sticks out into water is called a **peninsula.** (p. 76) A **peninsula** has water on three sides.

pictograph

A **pictograph** is a chart that shows information by using small pictures to stand for amounts. (p. 306) Each picture of a tomato can on the **pictograph** stood for ten tomatoes.

Key

= 10 cans

Number of Cans Collected

Class A   Class B   Class C   Class D   Class E

Pilgrim

A **Pilgrim** was one kind of colonist at Plymouth. (p. 232) The **Pilgrims** came to America to find religious freedom.

point of view

A way of looking at things is called a **point of view.** (p. 266) We each had a different **point of view** about which play to put on.

pole

North Pole

The place on the earth that is farthest north or south is a kind of **pole.** (p. 72) The North **Pole** and the South **Pole** are very cold.

South Pole

president

A **president** is the leader of a country or nation. (p. 138) John Adams was the second **President** of the United States.

price

The amount of money you pay to buy something is called **price.** (p. 180) The **price** of a box of cereal is $2.79.

producer

A **producer** is a person who makes or grows something. (p. 166) A baker is a **producer** of bread and rolls.

region

A region is an area that has some shared natural or human feature that sets it apart from other areas. (p. 92) The state of Iowa is in a plains **region.**

religious holiday

A special day that is important to people in a religion is called a **religious holiday.** (p. 146) In April, Buddhists celebrate the birthday of their founder on a **religious holiday** called Wesak.

responsibility

A **responsibility** is something that you should do. (p. 294) Everyone has the **responsibility** to obey the law.

right

A **right** is something you are free to do. (p. 293) You have the **right** to speak freely.

rule

A statement or an idea that tells people what they should or should not do is called a **rule.** (p. 29) One school **rule** says that you may not run in the hallway.

rural area

A **rural** area is a place that has fewer stores, schools, and homes than a city or suburb has. (p. 52) Farms and forests are found in **rural areas.**

savings account

A **savings account** is a service from a bank that allows people to earn interest on their money. (p. 182) Aki's **savings account** earned 11 cents in interest last month.

scale

0   miles   100

A line with a series of marks used to find distance on a map is a **scale.** (p. 202) Use a map **scale** to find how far apart two places are.

service

An activity that people do to help other people is called a **service.** (p. 173) A dentist provides a **service.**

settlement

A **settlement** is a small community started by people from another land. (p. 229) St. Augustine in Florida is the oldest lasting European **settlement** in America.

shelter

Something that protects or covers is called a **shelter.** (p. 160) Houses are kinds of **shelter.**

southeast

The direction between south and east is called **southeast.** (p. 82) Springfield, Illinois, is **southeast** of Des Moines, Iowa.

southwest

The direction between south and west is called **southwest.** (p. 82) Frankfurt, Kentucky is **southwest** of Columbus, Ohio.

specialize

Choosing to grow mainly one crop or to make only one main kind of product is to **specialize.** (p. 199) Farmers in Costa Rica **specialize** in growing bananas.

state

Part of a country is called a **state.** (p. 67) Ohio is one **state** of the 50 in the United States.

suburb

A **suburb** is a community near a city. (p. 46) Many people who live in a **suburb** work in the city.

symbol

A **symbol** is a picture, place, or thing that stands for something else. (pp. 34, 137) An eagle is a **symbol** of freedom.

tax

A **tax** is money that a government collects from citizens and businesses. (p. 287) A local government uses the **tax** money it collects to pay for services such as police.

technology

The use of science to make new things or to make things work better is called **technology.** (p. 260) People used **technology** to make faster and safer cars.

timeline

A **timeline** is an ordered group of words and dates that show when events happened. (p. 124) A **timeline** must be divided into equal parts.

Dan's Life History

0 1 2 3 4 5 6 7 8 9

Dan was born   Dan learned to read   Dan today

trade

The buying and selling of goods and services is called **trade.** (p. 197) People in this country take part in **trade** in many ways.

tradition

A **tradition** is something that people do the same way year after year. (p. 126) One **tradition** in my family is that you choose what is served for dinner on your birthday.

transportation

Any way of moving things or people from one place to another is called **transportation.** (p. 260) Cars are one kind of **transportation.**

urban area

An **urban area** is another word for city. (p. 44) An **urban area** has many buildings and people.

valley

The low land between mountains or hills is called a **valley.** (p. 75) A **valley** often has a river running through it.

vote

To **vote** means to show or make a choice for a leader or a law. (p. 308) You may **vote** for class president or team captain.

wants

Things that people would like to have, but do not have to have to stay alive are called **wants.** (p. 160) A new bike and roller skates are on my list of **wants.**

weather

What the air is like outside at any given time is called **weather.** (p. 84) Today the **weather** is warm and rainy.

world map

A **world map** is a flat drawing of the earth. (p. 32) You can see the whole earth at once on a **world map.**

Index

Page numbers with *m* after them refer to maps. Page numbers in italics refer to pictures.

Index

Acknowledgments

For each of the selections listed below, grateful acknowledgment is made for permission to excerpt and/or reprint original or copyrighted material, as follows:

Permissioned Material

Excerpts from "*The Fire Fighter's Job*" and "*Brave Fire Fighters,*" from *The Fire Station,* by Stuart A. Kallen. Copyright © 1997 by Abdo Consulting Group, Inc. Reprinted by permission of Abdo Publishing Company.

"*God Bless America,*" by Irving Berlin. © Copyright 1938, 1939, © copyright renewed 1965, 1966 by Irving Berlin. © Copyright assigned to the Trustees of the God Bless America Fund. International Copyright Secured. All Rights Reserved. Reprinted by permission of the Irving Berlin Music Company.

Lyrics from "I Live in a City," words and music by Malvina Reynolds. Copyright © 1961 by Schroder Music Co. (ASCAP) Renewed 1989. Used by permission. All rights reserved.

Excerpt from "Jackie Robinson's letter to Branch Rickey," [1950], by Jackie Robinson, Copyright © Jackie Robinson. Reprinted by permission of The Jackie Robinson Foundation.

Excerpt from *Journey to Ellis Island: How My Father Came to America,* by Carol Bierman with Barbara Hehner. Text copyright © 1998 by Carol Bierman. Jacket copyright © 1998 by The Madison Press Limited. Reprinted by permission of Madison Press Books.

"Maple Talk," from *Poems Have Roots,* by Lilian Moore. Text copyright © 1997 by Lilian Moore. Reprinted with the permission of Atheneum Books for Young Readers, an imprint of Simon & Schuster Children's Publishing Division and Marian Reiner for the author.

Excerpt from "North" ("The Young Woman and the Thunder Beings"), from *Between Earth & Sky: Legends of Native American Sacred Places,* by Joseph Bruchac. Text copyright © 1996 by Joseph Bruchac. Reprinted by permission of Harcourt, Inc. and Barbara S. Kouts Agency.

Excerpt from "Our Family Comes From 'Round the World," from *Fathers, Mothers, Sisters, Brothers,* by Mary Ann Hoberman. Copyright © 1991 by Mary Ann Hoberman. Reprinted by permission of Little, Brown and Company, (Inc.) and Gina Maccoby Literary Agency.

Excerpt from *Raising Cows on the Koebels' Farm,* by Alice K. Flanagan. Copyright © 1999 by Alice K. Flanagan and Romie Flanagan. All rights reserved. Reprinted by permission of Children's Press, an imprint of Scholastic Library Publishing, Inc.

"Recess Rules," from *Lunch Money,* by Carol Diggory Shields, illustrated by Paul Meisel. Text copyright © 1995 by Carol Diggory Shields. Illustrations copyright © 1995 by Paul Meisel. Used by permission of Dutton Children's Books, a division of Penguin Young Readers Group, a member of Penguin Group (USA) Inc., 345 Hudson Street, New York, NY 10014. All rights reserved.

Excerpt from *Sheep on the Farm,* by Mari C. Schuh. Copyright © 2002 by Capstone Press. All rights reserved. Reprinted by permission of Capstone Press.

Excerpt from *Sheep Out to Eat,* by Nancy Shaw, illustrated by Margot Apple. Text copyright © 1992 by Nancy Shaw. Illustrations copyright © 1992 by Margot Apple. Reprinted by permission of Houghton Mifflin Company.

Excerpt from "South" ("The Great Smokies"), from *Between Earth & Sky: Legends of Native American Sacred Places,* by Joseph Bruchac. Copyright © 1996 by Joseph Bruchac. Reprinted by permission of Harcourt, Inc. and Barbara S. Kouts Agency.

Index

Acknowledgments

Photography Credits

22–23 Kwane Zikomo/Superstock. 24 Gibson Stock Photography. 25 (l) Wes Thompson/Corbis; (r) Claver Carroll/Botanica/Getty Images. 26 Arthur Tilley/Taxi/Getty Images. 28 (l) SW Productions/Photodisc Red/Getty Images; (r) Rhoda Sidney/Photo Edit, Inc. 39 (c) Digital DataStream Inc/Paint Your Heart Out Tampa; (tr) Richard Steinmetz. 40–41 Courtesy of Maggie Cervantes. 44 Jeffrey Greenberg/Folio, Inc. 45 (tl) Owaki–Kulla/Corbis; (tr) Gibson Stock Photography. 46 (lc) Mark Richards/Photo Edit; (tr) Stephen Schauer/Stone/Getty Images. 48 (inset) Brinsley Ford Collection, London, UK/Bridgeman Art Library. 48–49 (bkgd) Andrew Gordon 2003/Panoramic Images. 50 Mitch Hrdlicka/Photodisc Green/Getty Images. 52 J Sohm/VOA LLC/Panoramic Images. 53 (br) Burwell/Folio Inc.; (c) Larry Lefever/Grant Heilman Photography. 54 (br) Jeff Green Berg/Photo Edit; (c) Alan Oddie/Photo Edit; (lc) Alec Pytlowany/Masterfile; (tr) Kitayama Sugi/Photonica. 55 (r) Rachel Epstein/Photo Edit; (inset) Richard Hamilton Smith/Corbis. 56 (b) David South/Image State–Pictor/PictureQuest; (t) Jon Riley Index Stock Imagery. 57 (l) TRBfoto/Photodisc/Getty Images; (r) TSUVOI/Masterfile. 62–63 (bkgd) Jesse Kalisher Gallery/Superstock; (inset) Palmer Kane Studios. 64 Mark Heifner/Pan Stock/Picturequest. 65 (l) Michael Melford/Imagebank/Getty Images;(r) Dan Budnik/Woodfin Camp & Associates. 70–71 (inset) NASA; (bkgd) Image produced by F. Hasler, M. Jentoft–Nilsen, H. Pierce, K. Palaniappan, and M. Manyin. NASA Goddard Lab for Atmospheres—data from National Oceanic and Atmospheric Administration NASA. 74–75 (b) Thomas Winz/Panoramic Images. 75 (t) Joseph Sohm/Corbis. 76 Tony Arruza/Corbis. 77 Terry Thompson/NGS Images.com/Panoramic Images. 78 Steve Dunwell/Getty Images. 79 Gibson Stock Photography. 80–81 (bkgd) Donovan Reese/Panoramic Images. 81 (tr) ABPL Image Library/Animals Animals/Earth Scenes. 86 (bl) Lonnie Duka/Index Stock Imagery; (br) Brad Wrobleski/Masterfile. 87 Alan and Sandy Carey/Photodisc Green/Getty Images. 94 C. C. Lockwood Bruce Coleman. 95 (tc) James Schwabel/Panoramic Images; (tl) New Moon/Panoramic Images; (tr) (c) HMCo./Photo Disk. 96 (br) Digital Vision. 96–97 (bkgd) Bryan Reinhart/Masterfile. 100 International Stock/Imagestate. 101 (br) Dwayne Newton/Photo Edit; (t) R. Ian Lloyd/Masterfile. 102 (l) Grant Heilman Photography; (r) Gibson Stock Photography. 104 Collart HERVE/Corbis. 105 (tl) Gibson Stock Photography; (tr) Gibson Stock Photography. 112–113 Banana Stock. 114 (r) Paul Barton/Corbis. 115 (r) Nik Wheeler/Corbis; (tl) Jerry Wachter/Photo Researchers. 116 Ariel Skelley/Corbis. 117 Tony Freeman/Photo Edit. 118 Lawrence Migdale. 119 (b) Rudi Von Briel/Index Stock Imagery, Inc.; (t) Dave G. Houser/Corbis. 120 Courtesy of Aparna Agrawal; 121 Courtesy of Maria Carter; 122–123 (bkgd) North Wind Picture Archive. 123 (c) Bettmann/Corbis. 124 (b) Burke/Triolo/Retrofile; (t) Myrleen Ferguson Cate/Photo Edit. 125 (c) Claudia Kunin/Corbis; (l) Horace Bristol/Corbis; (r) Don Mason/Corbis. 126 Paul Barton/Corbis; (tr) Creatas. 127 (bl) Creatas; (c) David Young-Wolff/Photo Edit. 129 (b) Mark Gibson/Index Stock; (tl) Superstock. 132–133 (b) Osamu Honda/AP World Wide Photo; 133 (tr) AP World Wide Photos. 136 (b) Superstock. 136–137 (tl) Ken Davies/Masterfile. 137 (br) Thinkstock/Getty Images. 138 (b) ro-ma stock/Index Stock Imagery, Inc. 139 (b) Leif Skoogfors/Woodfin Camp & Associates; (t) Danny Lehman/Corbis. 140 (b) Craig Aurness/Corbis; (t) Photolink/Photodisc Green/Getty Images. 141 James P. Blair/Corbis. 142–143 (b) Richard T. Nowitz/Corbis. 143 (r) Photodisc/Getty Images. 144 (frame) © HMCo./C. Squared Studios/Photodisc/Getty Images; (frame) © HMCo./C. Squared Studios/Photodisc/Getty Images; (l) Francis G. Mayer/Corbis; (r) Corbis.

145 Connie Ricca/Corbis. 146 (b) Roger Ressmeyer/Corbis; (c) Bob Krist/Corbis; (t) Michael Newman/Photo Edit. 147 Tim Boyle/Getty News and Sports/Getty Images. 148 (inset) Hulton Archive/Getty Images. 148–149 (bkgd) Walter P. Reuther Library, Wayne State University. 154 (c) Bob Thomas/Stone/Getty Images; (l) Jim Craigmyle/Corbis; (r) ImageState Pictor/PictureQuest. 156–157 David Young-Wolff/Photo Edit. 158 (l) Thinkstock/Getty Images; (r) Robert W. Ginn/Photo Edit. 160 Frank Siteman/Index Stock. 161 Superstock. 166 Photodisc/Getty Images. 167 LWA–Dann Tardif/Corbis. 168 (l) Jose Luis Pelaez, Inc./Corbis; (r) Ed Lallo/Index Stock Imagery. 169 (l) Stone/Getty Images; (r) Comstock Images. 172 Rogério Reis/Tyba Brazil Photos. 173 Corbis. 174 (bc) Scott Barrow/Image State; (r) photo Researchers. 175 (cr) Photodisc/Getty Images; (tl) Albert Gustaf Aristeded Edelfelt/SuperStock. 176 (c) Photodisc/Getty Images; (cr) Photodisc/Getty Images; (t) AP WorldWide Photos. 177 (l) Goldberg Diego/Corbis; (r) Goldberg Diego/Corbis. 178 G. K. & Vikki Hart/Getty Images. 181 (bl) Walter Hodges/Corbis; (br) © HMCo./C Squared Studios/Photodisc/Getty Images; (cr) Stone/Getty Images; (tl) John Coletti/Index Stock Imagery; (tr) Steve Cole/Photodisc/Getty Images. 182 Steve Dunwell/Indexstock Imagery. 183 Wonderfile. 188 (bl) Corbis; (br) Alan Pitcairn/Grant Heilman Photography; (c) Ed Young/Corbis. 189 (tr) Corbis. 191 (c) Taxi/Getty Images; (l) Ed Young/Corbis. 192 (l) Taxi/Getty Images; (r) Larry Lefever/Grant Heilman Photography. 193 David Young-Wolff/Photo Edit. 197 (tl) Allan Davey/Masterfile; (tr) Taxi/Getty Images. 198 (l) Dan Gair Photographic/Indexstock/PictureQuest; (r) Gibson Stock Photography. 208–209 John McGrail. 210 (l) The Bridgeman Art Library; (r) Maryann and Bryan Hempill/Index Stock. 211 (l) Bettmann/Corbis; (r) H.P. Merten/Zefa/Masterfile. 212 YVA Momatiuk & John Eastcott/Woodfin Camp & Associates. 216 (bl) Jules Frazier /Photodisc/Getty Images; (br) J. A. Kraulis /Masterfile; (tl) Scott T. Smith/Corbis; (tr) Marilyn "Angel" Wynn/NativeStock. 217 (tl) Marilyn "Angel" Wynn/Nativestock; (tr) Larry Ditto/Bruce Coleman. 222 The Granger Collection, New York. 223 The Bridgeman Art Library. 225 The Bridgeman Art Library. 226 Keren Su/Corbis. 228 John Anderson/Animals Animals. 242 Courtesy Don Troiani, Historical Military Imagebank. 244 Bettmann/Corbis. 245 (b) New York Historical Society/The Bridgeman Art Library; (t) Tom McHugh/Photo Researchers. 246 Photo Edit. 247 (tl) Massachusetts Historical Society. 248 Freelance Photography Guild/Corbis. 249 Rick Friedman/Corbis.

251 (c) Bettmann/Corbis; (frame) © HMCo./Image Farm; (l) Museum of the City of New York/Corbis; (r) Bettmann/Corbis. 253 The Bridgeman Art Library. 254 Bettman/Corbis. 255 Hulton Archive/Getty Images. 256 Bettman/Corbis. 257 Bettmann/Corbis. 258 (br) © HMCo./C Squared Studios/Photodisc/Getty Images; (cr) Bettman/Corbis. 259 Library of Congress. 260 Hulton–Deutsch Collection/Corbis. 262 (l) Underwood Photo Archives; (r) Minnesota Historical Society/Corbis. 263 (l) Underwood & Underwood/Corbis; (r) Courtesy of the Village of Plainfield. 264 (bl) Underwood & Underwood/Corbis; (tr) The Associated Publishers New York Public Library. 265 (bl) NASA/Science Source/Photo Researchers, Inc.; (tr) NASA. 266 (inset bl) George H.H. Huey/Corbis; (inset br) Bettmann/Corbis. 267 (bl) Bettmann/Corbis; (br) Mark M. Lawrence/Corbis; (cl) Hulton– Deutsch Collection/Corbis; (cr) Sean Sexton Collection/Corbis. 268 Tony Mc Grath/Hulton Archive/Getty Images. 269 (b) Underwood & Underwood Corbis; (t) Hulton Archive/Getty Images. 270 (br) Takaharu Yoshizawa/Photonica; (tl) Hot Idea's Collection/Index Stock. 271 Peter Cross's Collectiion/Index Stock. 272 (br) Museum of Mankind, London, UK/The Bridgeman Art

Library. 272–273 (bkgd) Galen Rowell/Corbis. 274 (l) British Museum London/Art Resource, NY; (lc) Bettmann/Corbis; (r) Joseph Sohm/Corbis; (rc) Richard T. Nowitz/Corbis. 275 (bl) Richard T. Nowitz/Corbis; (lc) Archivo Iconografico, S.A./Corbis; (rc) Burstein Collection/Corbis; (tl) Colin Garratt; Milepost 92 1/2/Corbis; (tr) Photonica. 276 The Granger Collection. 278–279 (l) Ariel Skelley/Masterfile. 280 (l) Michael Crabtree/Getty Images; (lc) Joseph Sohm Visions of America/Corbis. 280–281 (b)?? 281 (tr) Photodisc/Getty Images. 282 Richard Hutchings/Photo Edit. 283 Paul Colangelo/CORBIS. 286 (c) Elena Rooraid/Photo Edit; (l) ? (t)? 288–289 (bkgd) Skip Nall/Photodisc/Getty Images. 289 (inset) Chad Slattery/Stone/Getty Images. 301 Bonnie Kamin/Photo Edit. 302 ? 303 Jose Carillo/Photo Edit. 304 Reuters NewMedia Inc./Corbis. 304–305 Bettmann/Corbis. 309 (br) Bell/Folio Inc.; (cr) AP World Wide Photos; (tr) Office of the Mayor, Columbus Ohio. 310 (cl) Steven Begleiter/Image State; (cr) Jim and Mary Whitmer. 311 Rick Friedman/Corbis. 316? 317 ? 318 Peter Gridley/Taxi/Getty Images. 319 (bl) Peter Gridley/Taxi/Getty Images; (tr) Doug Armand/Stone/Getty Images. 320 (br) Ghislain & Marie David de ossy/Imagebank/Getty Images; (tr) Index Stock. 321 (bl) Wilfredo Lee/AP Wide World Photo; (tr) Richard Hutchings/Photo Edit. 322 (b) AFP Corbis. 323 Wally McNamee/Corbis. 324 Mark Wilson/Getty Images News and Sports/Getty Images. 325 (r) AFP/Corbis; (tl) Stephen Shaver, Pool/AP World Wide Photos. 326 (bl) Lawrence Migdale; (cl) Stockbyte/Punchstock. 327 (bc) David Young-Wolff/Photo Edit Inc; (c) Henryk T. Kaiser/Index Stock Imagery/Picturequest; (tc) Jack Star/Photolink/PhotoDisk/Getty Images; (tr) Dorian Weber/Index Stock Imagery.

Assignment Photography Credits

27 © HMCo./Ken Karp. 29 © HMCo./Ken Karp. 37 © HMCo./Ken Karp. 66–67 © HMCo./Ken Karp. 89–91 © HMCo./Ken Karp. 114 (l) © HMCo./Ken Karp. 128 © HMCo./Ken Karp. 130–131 © HMCo./Angela Coppola. 134 © HMCo./Ken Karp. 159 (r) © HMCo./Ken Karp. 180 © HMCo./Ken Karp. 184–185 © HMCo./Ken Karp. 187 © HMCo. 189 © HMCo./JP Maroot. 190 © HMCo./JP Maroot. 191 (r) © HMCo./JP Maroot. 227 (tr) © HMCO; (b) © HMCo./Ken Karp. 235–237 © HMCo./Ken Karp. 247 (bkgd) © HMCo./Angela Coppola. 252 © HMCo./Ken Karp. 267 © HMCo./Ken Karp. 284 © HMCo./Angela Coppola. 287 © HMCo./Angela Coppola. 292–293 © HMCo./Angela Coppola. 297–299 © HMCo./Angela Coppola. 308 © HMCo./Jade Albert. 312–315 © HMCo./Ken Karp. 328 © HMCo./Angela Coppola.

Illustration Credits

All cartographic maps done by Ortelious Design. 24 Ron Berg. 36 Alex Burnet. 43 Bob Depew. 46–47 Nathan Jarvis. 51 Christiane Beauregard. 58 Hector Borlasca. 60 Chris Lensch. 75–78 (borders) Sally Vitsky. 84 Mark and Rosemary Jarman. 86 Mark and Rosemary Jarman. 88–91 Steve Costanza. 92–93 Michael Maydak. 98 Jeffrey Mangiat. 103 Bob Depew. 108–109 Lucia Washburn. 151 Nathan Jarvis. 152 Promotion studios. 154 Nathan Jarvis. 162–163 Doris Barrette. 170–171 Len Ebert. 186 Peter Richardson. 194–195 Kathryn Mitter. 196 Lisa Campbell Ernst. 200 (br, cr) Jeffrey Mangiat. 204 Anthony Lewis. 214–215 Robert Van Nutt. 218–222 Richard Cowdrey. 230–233 Martha Aviles. 234–237 Jui Ishida. 239 Frank Riccio. 241 Viviana Diaz. 276 Leah Palmer Preiss. 284–285 ? 294 Kathi Ember. 297 ? 300 Ron Berg. 306 Jeff Mangiat. 310 Christiane Beauregard. 318 ? 328 ? 330 Nathan Jarvis.